WHO'S GONNA TAKE THE WEIGHT?

Other Books by Kevin Powell

In the Tradition: An Anthology of Young Black Writers
(1993; edited with Ras Baraka)

recognize (1995; poetry by Kevin Powell)

Keepin' It Real: Reflections on Race, Sex, and Politics
(1997; essays by Kevin Powell)

*Step into a World: A Global Anthology of the New Black
Literature* (2000; edited by Kevin Powell)

Who Shot Ya? Three Decades of Hiphop Photography
(2002; photographs by Ernie Paniccioli,
edited by Kevin Powell)

WHO'S GONNA TAKE THE WEIGHT?

Manhood, Race, and Power in America

Kevin Powell

THREE RIVERS PRESS • NEW YORK

Published by Three Rivers Press, New York, New York. Member of the Crown Publishing Group, a division of Random House, Inc.
www.randomhouse.com

THREE RIVERS PRESS and the Tugboat design are registered trademarks of Random House, Inc.

Some of the essays previously appeared in the following:
"The Breakdown" appeared in slightly different form as "Manhattan Breakdown, Harlem Healing" in *Code;* "Confessions of a Recovering Misogynist" appeared in *Ms;* Elements of "What Is a Man?" appeared as "Bury Me Like a G" in *Rolling Stone.*

Printed in the United States of America

Design by Lauren Dong

Library of Congress Cataloging-in-Publication Data
Powell, Kevin.
Who's gonna take the weight?: manhood, race, and power in America /
Kevin Powell.—1st ed.
1. African Americans—Social conditions—1975– 2. African
Americans—Intellectual life. 3. Hip-hop—Social aspects. 4. African
Americans—Civil rights. 5. Hip-hop—Political aspects. 6.
Masculinity—Political aspects—United States. 7. Power (Social
sciences)—United States. 8. United States—Race relations. 9. Powell,
Kevin. 10. African American journalists—Biography. I. Title.
E185.86 .P668 2003
305.896'073—dc21   2003003717

ISBN 0-609-81044-8

First Edition

For the people—young, old, and those not yet born

A traveler, who has just left a vast city, climbs the neighboring hill; as he goes farther off, he loses sight of the men whom he has just quitted; their dwellings are confused in a dense mass; he can no longer distinguish the public squares, and can scarcely trace out the great thoroughfares; but his eye has less difficulty in following the boundaries of the city, and for the first time he sees the shape of the whole.

—Alexis de Tocqueville, *Democracy in America*

Standin' at the crossroad
    I tried to flag a ride
Didn't nobody seem to know me
    everybody pass me by

—Robert Johnson, "Cross Road Blues"

am i headed for the same brick wall
is there anything i can do
about anything at all

—Ani DiFranco, "Fuel"

THANK YOU'S

THANK YOU TO Chris Jackson, my editor, for pushing me to complete this book. I could not have done it without you, and I mean that. Thank you to everyone at Three Rivers Press / Random House for supporting this project. Thank you, as always, to Andrew Wylie, Jeff Posternak, and the good people at the Wylie Agency. Thank you, in no particular order, to the late Weldon Irvine, James Mtume, Dr. bell hooks, Dr. Jerry Ward, the late Tupac Shakur, Robyn Rodgers (DJ Reborn), Faatima Muhammad, Ernie Paniccioli, (Brother) Bob Davis and all the folks at American Program Bureau, Davey D., Sharonda Simmons, Kevin Chen, Alec Ross, April Silver, Jabari Asim, Dr. Mark Anthony Neal, Taigi Smith, Angela Brown, Zac McDaniels, Lauren Summers, Jan Summers, Dr. Arnold Lehman, Howard Pitsch, Tracy Alexander, Michael Cummings, Hazel Rowley, Andrea Pinkney, Radcliffe Bailey, Deborah Willis, Leigh Savidge, Chuck D., Russell Simmons, Fatima Robinson, Jacque Reid, Ben (Chavis) Muhammad, Michael Eric Dyson, Pearl Cleage, Nikki Giovanni, Charles Harris, Harry Allen, Dr. Blue Maas, Greg Tate, Michael Cohen, Baraka Sele, Dr. Kamau

Thank You's

Kokayi, Bahia Ramos, Nikki "Cynical" Smith, Chie Davis, Eternal Polk, Jessica Care Moore, Herb Boyd, Don Rojas, Penny Wrenn, Darwin Beauvais, Michael Datcher, Dr. Maryemma Graham, the late Lisa Sullivan, Billy "Upski" Wimsatt, Aishah Shahidah Simmons, Tyree Simmons (DJ Drama), Toni Scott, Lisa-Erika James, Alvin Starks, Ama Codjoe, Aaron Burrison, Eisa Ulen, Raymond O'Neal, Toni Blackman, Mahogany Browne, DJ Kuttin Kandi, Kool Herc, Afrika Bambaataa, Jorge "Fabel" Pabon, Tony Medina, Willie Perdomo, Angelica Patterson, Renaldo Davidson, Kenji Jasper, Conrad Muhammad, Keith Clink-scales, Miles Marshall Lewis, John McGregor, and Knox Robinson for the invaluable life lessons these past few years, even if some of y'all don't know or realize what you taught me. *I do.* . . . Ms. Conya Doss, thank you for the prayers and the great conversations during the last lap of this book. To all my peeps in ghetto villages everywhere— I'm representin' for all y'all, aiight? And thank you to my moms for teaching me more about manhood than any man could have. I ain't never gonna let you down, ma.

CONTENTS

PROLOGUE

IN THE SUMMER OF 2001, I WAS ARRESTED FOR DE-
stroying the sunglasses of another writer, another Black
male. You see, I felt this writer had previously disrespected me on a few occasions by bad-mouthing me to
colleagues we had in common. What really incensed me is
that I had literally met this individual when he first arrived
in New York City a few years before, and taken the time, as
I always try to do, to offer some advice about living and
working in this overwhelming metropolis. Now I heard
he'd been dissing me.

I will be brutally honest here and say that leading up to
this specific incident, I had had a few other confrontations,
in one form or another, over the course of a two- to three-
year period, with other men of color in my generation
whom I felt had disrespected me in some way. There was
the old-school hip-hop dancer I blasted on the Internet
about his and his wife's bitter contempt for my work and
my various roles within the hip-hop community. There
was another writer who had penned a negative review of
an anthology I had edited—of which he had wanted to be
a part—whom I stepped to at a corner in Greenwich Vil-

lage in New York City, all but threatening to beat him down if he ever violated me in that manner again and, for good measure, hock-spitting my aversion for him in his direction. And there was a former coworker from my days at *Vibe* with whom I got into a physical altercation outside of a holistic soul-food restaurant in Brooklyn because I felt he too had been disrespectful to my being.

So, clearly, I was on edge when I saw this writer at a Brooklyn street festival that summer day. I approached him to ask what was the deal. At first I was calm, but this writer was smug to the point of condescension and was hiding his eyes behind expensive, mirrored lenses. And he said to me, as I was asking why he insisted on sullying my name, that he *knew* me, that I was no gangsta. If there is one thing that has always gotten my goat, it is when people who have never spent any quality time around me proclaim in that patronizing, tongue-in-cheek way that they *know* me. Thus I pulled the thug from my back pocket, and quicker than you could say Suge Knight, I snatched the sunglasses from this writer's face, told him if he ever talked to me like that again he would receive a severe whooping, and I refused to return his shades as he followed me around the street festival near tears, begging for his high-priced frames. I took perverse pleasure in watching him sweat and plead, for he represented something I did not like about several professional, middle-class men I knew, as well as their bohemian backpacker cousins, something that seemed plastic, contrived, shallow, weak—and I was determined to teach this writer a lesson. I ultimately broke his glasses in half and threw them into a sewer.

Within a week the police made numerous stops at my home, pressing my doorbell at different hours of the day and night, very obviously looking for me and leaving a business card with instructions to call each time. I ducked and dodged the police for several days before finally phoning them. What choice did I have, really? The Brooklyn grapevine had informed me that this writer had pressed charges. Whoever I spoke with over the phone told me I had to come down to the 88th precinct in Brooklyn without delay. As soon as I got there, I was immediately arrested, although I was not handcuffed or placed in a holding cell. I think the only thing that kept me from spending the weekend in the Brooklyn Detention Center was the fact that the detective who booked me, a middle-aged Black woman, bought my harangue about the police wasting their time on me when there were real crooks to catch, and that she would thereby be participating in the march of yet another Black male through the justice system. No matter, I was held for a good ten hours as a check was run on my "criminal record," and it was then and there, as I waited, and waited, and waited, that I began to play back in my troubled mind all the arguments and fights I had had with schoolmates, friends, rivals, authority figures; as well as the arrests and court appearances as a teen, as an early twenty-something, and now, in my mid-thirties.

I thought about this one particular appearance in front

of a Black female judge in my hometown of Jersey City, when it looked as if I was heading straight to a home for wayward youth. This judge knew that arguing and fighting were my way of dealing with every single matter, how it had something to do with going to four grammar schools and three high schools, and how this behavior, this very reactionary behavior, had forced my mother, who raised me alone in dreadful poverty, to time and again miss work for visits to my school and those agonizing trips to juvenile court. I don't know why I was never sent away as an adolescent because I surely tempted fate many, many times. I was bad, very bad, so bad that my mother often said to me "I don't think you are going to make it," which is a Black mother's way of saying she believes her Black son is not going to live a long, fruitful life. Perhaps that Black female judge felt the same, for I recall her giving me a stern lecture as if she saw something in me I did not yet see in myself, how her final words to me were "I hope to never see you again—" That judge's words clanged around the corridors of my mind as I waited at the 88th precinct. I wondered to myself if something might pop up in that detective's "computer search" that I had previously ignored or forgotten, some warrant, some missed court appearance, *anything*. The cockiness wrenched itself from my flesh as a hardened, dried-up scab would, and I sat slumped in a chair in that detective's office, certain that I had done something to ruin my life, yet again—

After much posturing and lying about what happened between myself and that writer to friends and colleagues, to my lawyer, I finally wound up in court two weeks after the destruction of the World Trade Center in New York City on September 11, 2001. Between my arrest that summer day and September 11, I had unlimited time to meditate on my actions leading up to my indiscretion and the plethora of dramatic wrecks I had driven myself into in the decade or so since I had appeared on the first season of MTV's *The Real World;* and during my very successful but also very tumultuous stint as a senior writer at *Vibe* magazine.

To be sure, I had, and have, spent the better part of my post-college life growing up in the public eye, with my shameful warts, big and ugly, looming there for the world to see; and it has been a mighty battle trying to be a man, a Black man, a human being, a responsible and consistent human being, as I have interfaced with my past and with my personal demons, with friends and lovers, with enemies and haters. As Tupac Shakur once famously said to me, "There is no place called careful." On the one hand, Tupac was right: There is not much room for error in America if you are a Black male in a society ostensibly bent on profiling your every move, eager to capitalize on your falling into this or that trap, particularly keen to swoop down on your self-inflicted mishaps. But by the same token, Tupac was wrong: There can be a place called careful, once one becomes aware of the world one lives in, its potential, its limitations, and if one is willing to struggle to create a new model, some new and alternative space outside and away from the larger universe, where one can be free enough to comprehend that even if the world seems aligned against you, you do not have to give the world the rope to hang you with. I have had the noose around my neck more times than I care to admit, and for whatever magical reasons, I have escaped the lynching each time.

That is precisely what I was thinking as I sat, slumped, in a back-row bench in that Brooklyn criminal courtroom on that late September day, watching one Black or Latino young male after another being paraded in front of a middle-aged White male judge—a judge who could, would, determine the life journey of us all, for the next day, the next week, the next year, the next decade, and, for a few, the remainder of their natural lives. I could not help but ask myself, "Why are you here, Kevin Powell? Why did you allow a feeling of *disrespect* to crawl so deeply into your fiber that you felt compelled to respond to it, to the person hurling the contempt, even if it meant the possibility of jeopardizing or losing your own life in the process?" Or, better yet, "What kind of power do you have that you are so utterly powerless when it comes down to controlling your own emotions, your own pain, your own rage?"

When my time finally came to stand before the judge, I was both nervous and embarrassed. Nervous because I was certain the judge would ask me why I had previously lied about destroying that writer's glasses. Embarrassed because a few folks who worked in the courtroom recognized me from MTV and other television appearances, and one even asked if he could have my autograph afterward. The judge ordered me to pay for the sunglasses, which I agreed to do, and he said to me, eerily, as that judge had said to me when I was a teen, "I hope to never see you again—"

And like that, I was out into the streets walking as fast as I could, away from that criminal court building, vowing, once and for all, to work through my issues of respect and disrespect, of the feeling of powerlessness that has led men like me to believe that if we do not respond to every slight, threat, attack, innuendo, defeat, if we do not fight back, harass, brutalize, *win*, then we are somehow less than men. As I trekked back to my apartment in Brooklyn, I thought of this in the larger context of the American response to the September 11 attacks on the Twin Towers: how almost instantly the first thought, the first reaction, was to respond with violence, to attack, to scour the earth until every "terrorist" was found and destroyed. How the American empire has not been shy about the need to oust or kill certain leaders of certain countries (if you are the lone superpower on the planet at the dawn of this new millennium, then you certainly are an empire, and whatever that word conjures in the raw, unchecked imagination of the powerful). Of how this nation was founded on the violent taking of Native Americans' land, of the violent enslavement of African people—my ancestors—how people we call Mexican or Chicano saw parts of what is now the American Southwest, including President George W. Bush's home state of Texas, fall to the violence of American interests. And what of the women who have been assaulted throughout American history, from Black female slaves to some girl somewhere in America who is being raped right as you are reading these words, her screams silent, the rehabilitation for her mind and soul more than likely never to happen. Or what of those in the homosexual community who must deal with both verbal and physical violence, of people who feel homosexuals are going to hell because of their sexual orientation, who feel that by verbally or physically pummeling them that perhaps they will return to their "natural state" as heterosexuals.

These thoughts crept into my mind because it was clear to me, immediately following the court appearance, that no matter my protestations and statements to the contrary, I had acted the part of a very typically American male on many levels, that my response to that writer, to those other men, was exactly the way I had been instructed to respond practically from my first steps out of the cradle: that "real men" deal with their tribulations through force, domination, elimination, violence. I felt sick and more embarrassed, for I've spent a good deal of my adult life grappling with what it means to be a man, and I had slipped badly, yet again. But, for some reason, this slip hit me harder because, post-September 11, the idea that someone bad-mouthing me could occupy more than a tiny space in my head appeared to be implausible. In light of the death and mayhem consuming the earth every single day, what did it matter what someone thought of me, especially if that someone was not a close friend or a loving relative? Hell, I should have asked that question pre-September 11, given how sensitive I have been, for such a long time, to poverty, hunger, homelessness, and, truly, any form of oppression, and oppression's too-many-to-count victims around the globe. And although I understood, and understand, the thirst for revenge and justice many Americans have demanded as a result of the nearly three thousand lives lost on September 11, I could not, and cannot, look myself in the mirror and say, finally, that violence is the solution to every problem, or, indeed, to *any* problem. Not any longer. For those who commit acts of violence, be it as an aggressor or a defender, not only hurt and destroy the recipients of that violence, they hurt and destroy themselves as well. How can anyone be whole after that, or be healthy spiritually, psychologically?

This is something I hope we humans permit to marinate in our psyches as we sprint through the first chapters of the twenty-first century. One hundred years ago, W. E. B. DuBois stated in his classic tome, *The Souls of Black Folk*, that the problem of the twentieth century was the problem of the color line. I submit, one hundred years later, that the problem in the world today is race *and* sex *and* class operating in tandem to control, bamboozle, violate, divide, and conquer the majority of us while a certain elite and wealthy minority gets to win in the largest possible meaning of the term "win." This minority will have the everyday people among us wrestle over emotionally charged issues like affirmative action—Is it quotas? Is it favoritism, reverse discrimination? Meanwhile, we ignore the ample proof that President Bush is clearly a beneficiary of the peculiar institution of *White* affirmative action: His White-skin privilege coupled with his opulent bloodline has afforded him extraordinary opportunities a male or female of a comparable demeanor and intelligence would never get—*never*. That conundrum aside, it should be duly noted that America is not the terribly undemocratic nation it once was, pre–Civil Rights Movement; nor is America the democracy it declares itself to be, either. Just ask the good people in Florida who did not vote for Mr. Bush in the 2000 general election.

So, my mission at this moment in my life journey is to rise above the slings and arrows of outrageous fortune; to vaccinate myself against that mental terrorism germ known as self-hatred, hatred of people who look like me, and the hatred of individuals or groups irrespective of who they are; and to be a truth-seeker and a truth-teller, not just for myself as a man, or as a Black man, and not just for Black people, but for the human race. In other words, I do not want to be stuck on the treadmill of emotional under-development and confusion forever. For sure, we human beings—each and every one of us—have to ask some very profound questions as we spin into more random acts of violence, more wars, more dissections, more globalization, more fear, and more loathing, and more individual and collective tragedies: Do I want to be typical and predictable and a blind follower of who I am told to be, and what I am supposed to do, or do I want to be a different kind of human being with a different sense of humanity, some purpose greater than surviving day to day, year to year, or from the accumulation of one material gain to the next? If there is no other lesson from September 11, there is this: When we die, we will not be able to take any of these material items with us nor will it matter what our status was in this lifetime. What we will be able to leave as our true and lasting legacy is a humanity rooted in self-love and a love for life, not a lust for the vicious cycles of death and madness so many of us have become accustomed to.

I don't pretend to be a perfect man, but I do ask myself the hard questions at every turn. And I do own my backwardness sooner or later, which means, in due time, I apologized to each of the men I had a beef with these past few years, including that writer who had me arrested. I may never agree with the actions and reactions of heads whose sensibilities and worldviews are far removed from mine, but I must at least respect their humanity, even as I speak my truths uncensored, and with no warning sticker. That said, it is no easy task to take the weight of one's own life and scrutinize it, front to back, top to bottom, inside out, and say, humbly, I must do better, I must be better, I must get better. But, I must, and *we* must.

THE BREAKDOWN

And we are programmed to self-destruct, to fragment.

—Jayne Cortez, "There It Is"

A FEW SHORT YEARS AGO, I WANTED TO END MY life. Suicide, yeah. You see, there is nothing worse nor more humiliating than to move to a metropolis like New York, become a writer both prolific and known during your very hip twenties, then lose it all—your cushy magazine job, your phat apartment, your instant access to money—by the age of thirty. I suffered through this period privately, telling a small knot of comrades of my predicament, while feigning sanity to others. That I am able to write this essay is testament to how far I have come since falling so low. I am not remotely confident where to start other than to quote F. Scott Fitzgerald who said famously, "All life is a process of breaking down."

Like Fitzgerald's roaring 1920s, the naughty '90s were my time to live and play irresponsibly. Upon moving to upper Manhattan—Harlem—from Jersey City, New Jersey, my hometown, in August 1990, I wrote in my diary, somewhat egotistically and in spite of my few years of toiling in obscurity as a freelance news reporter, that I wanted to be remembered as one of the best, and best-known, writers of my generation. As the elders say, be careful what you ask for.

Two years after my unheralded arrival on Manhattan's shores, I would be drafted to costar on MTV's hugely popular docu-soap *The Real World*, and soon thereafter I found myself writing the cover story for a new magazine founded by Quincy Jones named *Vibe*. I had become a staff writer with a national byline and face recognition at twenty-six. I wore this freshly minted notoriety akin to how a homeboy wears his straight-outta-the-box Timberland boots. I admired it in the mirror. I scrubbed that notoriety regularly. I deemed my self-generated franchise better than anyone else's. And I got caught up in the hype of the entertainment industry: the fluffy parties, the air kisses, the synthetic let's-do-lunch rhetoric, the rubbing of slippery elbows with icons like Spike Lee, Tommy Hilfiger, General Colin Powell, and many, many others. At *Vibe*, the demand to produce articles like a well-oiled machine wore on me. I binged on liquor to keep the motor going; I drank more liquor to make it stop. I did not take a legitimate vacation during my four-year association with the glossy. I felt guilty for thinking of one, and I found myself becoming an insomniac who slept by inhaling loads of liquor or alcohol-laced NyQuil.

Then, in May 1996, I was fired.

IN THE NATURE of these things, my firing was the twin two-edged sword to my hiring. When I started at *Vibe* it was a magazine that promised to boldly, beautifully show-case the journalistic element of the culture I lived and breathed, which I'll roughly define by that elusive term of art: hip-hop. But almost from the start it betrayed the source of its power. Many of us people of color at this os-tensibly urban, people-of-color magazine were miffed that management could never seem to find "qualified" Black editors. Moreover, it bothered us that while the col-ored folks—chiefly the mostly female cadre of editorial assistants—carried workloads comparable to those of the White men at the monthly, the salaries and perks were hardly in the spirit of egalitarianism. Among ourselves, at the water cooler, outside the office during lunch breaks, or even within earshot of some of our White coworkers and superiors, we began mocking the *Vibe* headquarters as "da plantation," because, as coarse as it sounds, we felt like the latest in history's line of slaves, picking the cotton only to watch the masters reaping the profits from our labor.

This wasn't the way it was supposed to be. We were supposed to be a chic, multicultural collection of the best and the brightest, inventing a way to *do* hip-hop in words on the pages of a glossy, national magazine on a weekly basis. That's what Quincy himself promised at the maga-zine's launch (geez, how rapidly I figured out that Q may have been the founder, but it was not him running things day to day). But the scene lost its sexy allure—with a quickness—once it became plain as the African nose on my face that *Vibe,* for all its freshness, was run the old-fashioned way, by a strictly enforced racial hierarchy with

White male editors at the top, including a grumpy old dinosaur that Time Warner (the original owner of *Vibe*) deposited as the editorial "consultant" for the magazine. But this stifling hierarchy was more than just business as usual to me; it was patently obscene in the context of the culture we were ostensibly representing, not to mention that more than a few of those White male editors were ridiculously incompetent and, we suspected, only using *Vibe* as a launching pad to "better opportunities" at mainstream White-oriented periodicals. On the other hand, for most of us Black and Brown writers, we knew damn well that *Vibe* was as good as it was ever going to get. We were committed because the magazine was more than just representative of our culture; we had started to see it as the only refuge for our professional survival.

The old dinosaur habitually marked up pieces with a pen adroit at minimizing commentary that flirted with race and racism in America. Indeed, there was a time when one could write an article for *Vibe* and after it left one's Black hands, no Black hands—not those of the editor, the researcher, the copy editor, the editor in chief, or the consultant—would touch that article until another set of Black hands purchased the magazine. It would be years later before *Vibe* began to consistently hire editors of color, including for the post of editor in chief—a change brought about largely because of the unrest we sparked during those first years, I feel.

The potency of our sense of injustice—my sense of injustice—might seem silly to some, but to think of this as just one writer's problem at one magazine is to miss the larger point. Yes, this is the story of my personal breakdown, but it's also the story of the maddening endurance of White-skin privilege—even in as unlikely an arena as hip-hop—and how this persistent, insidious force worms its way into lives and psyches, forcing us to deal with it, to take a position on it, to make choices of consequence even when our judgment isn't clear. Sometimes, when we're tired from the fight, it can drive us crazy. Most of my White peers saw nothing wrong with the *Vibe* power structure, which spoke to how comfy they were in their White-skin privilege. How could I be mad at that? If your whole life has been spent on top with doors flung open for you at every turn, regardless of whether you are qualified to go through those doors or not, why on God's vast earth would you *think* to challenge something like that? For in defying that, you would be messing with the very basis of your day-to-day existence. This realization became a hot coal in my chest every time my disgust with the editorial plantation was dismissed by my White colleagues.

One of their key arguments involved conjuring up the distorted legacy of integration, the hideously naive or hideously cynical notion that merely having people of different colors in proximity at the table of humanity would be sufficient to eradicate centuries of ingrained White supremacy. What is conveniently omitted is that Dr. King, the alleged architect of integration, by the end of his life was calling for economic justice (remember the Poor People's Campaign, beloved?) and was rethinking integration as the best route for Black America, especially if it meant Blacks would remain mired in bottomless self-hatred and confusion, fundamentally powerless. I count myself among those who believe the Civil Rights Movement was about changing policies of legal desegregation, freeing African Americans to exercise their birthright of free movement in this social order without the fear of attack or retribution. In other words, to realize, without legal restraint, the full experience of human freedom. At some point in the transmitting of the civil rights narrative the script was flipped: The hardheaded fight against segregation was swapped for the warm symbolism of integration. Over time, this symbolic integration has found its goal in the triumph of the myth of multiculturalism. But even though the colors of the rainbow can all chill together—at least in Gap commericals—they are not all sharing *in the power*. So what's the point of multiculturalism if it is reduced to folks eating each other's foods, marrying each other, having multiracial children, and proclaiming myopically that interracial relationships, be they friendships or loveships, will rid the country of its historically paralyzing racial quagmire? Or *is* that the point? As presently practiced in the majority of American circles, this kind of Happy Meal multiculturalism allows us to avoid yet again the necessity of scrutinizing, in a grab-the-collar, eyeball-to-eyeball manner, the power dynamic this country was founded on.

America *was* "multicultural" right from the very beginning, given the presence of Native Americans (the original owners of this land you call your land), Europeans, and captured Africans. America is a mulatto family, has always been, and will always be—this is neither news nor a cause for celebration. But why must the head of the household ceaselessly be a White male calling the shots? Rich White males are still the straws that stir the drink, and the rest of us are supposed to just smile and go along for the ride, content that we have employment, 401K plans, and health benefits. Even if we *don't* have these middle-class accoutrements—even if we only see them on TV—we are supposed to be content that those dreadful For Coloreds Only signs have disappeared. But while the physical signs have come down—after much protest and much bloodshed—the signs never came down in our shared psyche. Buried in the mud of our collective brain, the wriggling worm of White supremacy, White entitlement, White power is still there.

AND THIS WAS, for me, the crux of the matter. Thus who cares if it was the same poor Black and Latino people Dr. King was attempting to help at the end of his life—the ones left behind by the gold rush of integration (oh, the contemporary Black middle class has a heavy cross to bear for its unapologetic abandonment of the Black poor)— who created hip-hop culture as a response to their alienation, their isolation, their invisibility? Who cares if these poor Black and Latino people were simply attempting to make something out of nothing, to create power for themselves, alchemizing it from the minimal resources at their disposal in their very limited and forgotten world? And who cares if these same poor Black and Latino people would, by laying their souls and their lives and their genius on the line, launch a cultural revolution that would inspire *two* American generations (and counting) and youth across the globe? If you think hip-hop does not rule the cultural world, you'd better look again. In the beginning, these wretched of the earth took very basic tools—two turntables, a microphone, spray paint and markers, cardboard from the corner store, and linoleum from their mother's kitchen floor—and hewed the four fundamental elements of hip-hop practiced by four new kinds of urban artists: the DJ, the MC, the dancer, and the graffiti writer.

I was one of those young people who participated in this thing, this energy, before it was even categorized as "hip-hop." I learned any and all inner-city dances; scratched my multifarious nicknames into my school desk, on lockers, or on walls; mouthed the lyrics of the hot MCs of the day, flashing my hands to mark out the beat in the air; and tinkered with the DJ's equipment, albeit not very well. As a jazz connoisseur is passionate, I am passionate: I live and die for hip-hop culture and am a self-described hip-hop head. Hell, I am hip-hop, to bite rapper KRS-One's brash declaration. And hip-hop is mine. I earned it, just like a million other ghetto bastards left behind in the '70s and '80s.

I remember when only a few brave White people hung around hip-hop clubs like the Latin Quarters, Union Square, and the Rooftop, while most condescendingly dismissed it as nothing more than a passing fad. They were dead wrong. Hip-hop is what rock and roll and jazz once were: the popular American music that owns the epoch, that speaks to the spirit of the generation that gave it birth and the generation that grew up with it. And like those other, earlier art forms, this culture, too, must have mouthpieces—writers, critics, radio DJs—to track its evolutions and revolutions, describe it, analyze it, celebrate it, and try to understand it. *Vibe, The Source, XXL, Redeye, The Fader, Murder Dog*—these and other fanzines were born as a corollary of hip-hop. Don't get it twisted, yo. The media was the tail, hip-hop was the dog.

And it was this background that I brought with me to *Vibe.* Yes, I, a poor colored lad from the gutter, was elated that I had a job writing about something as natural to me as the air puncturing my nostrils. On the other hand, I also wanted more than just a taste of power because, for Christ's sake, *we* created this culture.

But *we* had no major clout at *Vibe.* I remember being told repeatedly, primarily on those days when it was clear that I was not happy, by the White folks and the Black CEO who assiduously barked the company line: "Kevin, these business affairs are not your worry, just write." In a way they were right: I was a writer, and if a writer has any right to that title, then he or she must learn to sense deception. And I could sense clearly that *we* were not being treated as equals, that we were being duped and the people doing the duping were convinced that they'd pulled the wool tightly over our eyes without us noticing.

***

AMERICA HAS A legacy of deceit masquerading as history. Conceivably we can overcome our fear of the past and actually discuss racism intimately, but first we must be willing to discuss what happened to the Native Americans and those captured Africans before, during, *and* after slavery (anybody out there down to define *reparations*?). Meanwhile, our nation of millions partakes in this grand scheme, and in the immortal, stuttered speech of the eternally battered and bruised Rodney King, we implore, lips greasy, mournful: "Can we all just get along?" We imagine that everything is swell because to begin unraveling the layers of deceit and violence and theft that brought us to this comfy present would require us to open our eyes to a singular horror and fall to our knees in shame. I recall those bare, empty stares of most of my White *Vibe* cohorts vividly. Those stares said, in effect, *We do not understand what* that *has to do with* this, *and besides, there is nothing we can do about it, and for that matter, why don't you just lighten up a little?*

Afresh the buck is passed from that generation to this generation. As we are told, as them Negroes were told in Alabama and Mississippi in the 1960s, *go slow*. No one, beloved, is willing to carry the weight of this racial trick bag. The scenes have changed, but the scenes remain, inexplicably, the same. The innocent children assert, in unison, *By gosh, the office* is *diverse, so what could possibly be the matter?* The matter is that the natives—as in those tragically racist Bob Hope–Bing Crosby flicks—will shortly get restless. This is not about one writer, one magazine, one culture. This is about power and its consequences: Who wields it and who does not?

The entertainment industry is one of the few places—along with sports, the Black church, and the drug hustle on the block—where folks have the impression that Black people have achieved power and wealth by virtue of our stunning, swaggering overrepresentation and the gaudy amounts of money evidently generated. But real power doesn't necessarily follow appearance. What we have is a presence, but only if your name happens to be Russell Simmons or Oprah Winfrey or Bill Cosby is that presence accompanied by even a small amount of power. Power means the ability to say what can and cannot go in a national magazine with millions of readers, in editorials *and* in ads. Power means the ability to say which artists will be supported by a record company, how big those artists become, and why. Power means the ability to delegate the mining of America's ghettos for musical talent to desperate dark-skinned "entrepreneurs," providing them with the illusion of a label deal and corporate support, but never letting these glorified miners get their hands on the precious yield of their work—the masters—and all the while keeping a firm grip on the means of production and distribution.

Expanding the conversation, power means the ability to say what sort of textbooks are coming into the schools in your community, which, for all intents and purposes, signifies the power to determine *whose* education your children will be receiving, from what angle, and to what effect on your children's self-image. A number of these same children will one day aspire to be rap stars or some general cog in the entertainment empire and see nothing wrong with denigrating their people (and themselves) as "niggas" and "bitches" because their marvelously imaginative school system never bothered to teach them anything about American history from viewpoints other than that of the heroic Europeans and their descendants. Indeed, what other people in the history of this planet have been so miseducated that they see nothing wrong with publicly identifying themselves as "niggas" and "bitches" (under the pretext of keepin' it real)? That self-hatred is then digitized on compact disc and shipped worldwide by multinational conglomerates—Sony, Bertelsmann, Vivendi Universal, AOL Time Warner, et alia—until the whole world can discover and emulate our self-hatred, thinking that these words manifest who we think we are. *Niggas and bitches . . .*

That is power, my friend. Meanwhile, we are expected to be content with overpriced jewelry, clothes with some designer's name emblazoned all over them, easy access to parties, book deals, guest appearances on MTV or VH1 (it is so so def to be an in-demand young Black writer these days with nothing, fuh shizzle, to say), free CDs and T-shirts, an expense account for all those lunches and dinners and trips, and a pipeline to all the liquor and marijuana and Ecstasy humanly consumable while etching another saga in the life of "the industry." But even in the haze of my drinking sprees and ego rides, I smelled a rat. Something was rotten in Gotham, and all the pats on the back and nice liberal smiles could not erase that certainty. This multicultural mecca was a vacuous hell once my heart aligned itself with my head and I saw, suddenly, a crystallized truth: I was more than just a happy darkie thrilled to have a gig. Or, as rapper Chuck D. has said, maybe a bit too bluntly for the taste buds of the hypersensitive, *slavery* was a job, with work hours and a daily regimen, once you stop to contemplate that peculiar institution. Here I was, a twentieth-century slave ready to break north, but completely unable to rid myself of the mental shackles implanted by the high life of the industry.

I WILL NOT front, though: I got mad love for some of the White colleagues I had at *Vibe*—Jonathan Van Meter (he gave me my big break by hiring me), Alan Light, and Rob Kenner, among others—but I also know that they may never understand why some of us felt the way we did. How could they, in spite of whatever love they may have for individual Black people or for Black music and Black culture? I am checking for more than an appreciation, friend. I wanted to see us in on the major decision making of *Vibe*, on both the editorial and business sides, and I could not understand why *they* could not understand why we were pissed by the mirage of progress.

Is this what the Civil Rights Movement was for? To leave our Black-run institutions—our neighborhoods, our schools, our law firms, our newspapers and magazines, our banks, our insurance companies, our hotels, and so on, where we ran things, where there was some semblance of self-determination and power—so that we could be in an integrated heaven where we can't even decide what time to go to lunch? What a conundrum, as has been said by another writer in another time. All of this troubled me greatly; I knew I was trapped by the game, I began hating my job, and I became increasingly hostile toward my employers. Yes, I had had temper tantrums before: Lawd knows up until this showdown I had often acted a fool up at *Vibe*, screaming at folks, hurling thinly veiled threats, my social skills, back then, about as refined as Bill O'Reilly's or the latest, hottest rapper with a long rap sheet. But now things were different, at least I thought so, because I figured the work I had done, the many major cover stories, the glory I had helped to bring to *Vibe,* meant I had a voice, some juice, some, well, power. I felt my feet slipping, my head sinking under the waves of my own rage. Determined to change things, the coloreds secretly planned a revolt . . . sort of. As the most visible voice at *Vibe,* I was to lead the protest. But before anything constructive could be done, I allowed the anger, the exhaustion, and the frustration to get to me, and one day I just lost it.

It was a Friday, I know that, but it's a blur in my memory no matter how many times I rerun the tape. I was in *Vibe*'s bright, modern offices, struggling with ancient problems—both within me and around me—when my words, my language felt suddenly, hideously impotent, not up to the task of navigating a solution. I felt myself crashing against the same old rocks, and that hot coal in my chest glowed brighter. Finally I couldn't control it anymore. I cursed out several staff members—Black, White, whomever, it didn't make a difference at that point—and I had to be physically restrained. Later that day I was called in front of the magazine's senior staff after everyone else had gone home for the weekend and was unceremoniously terminated—told, among other things, that I was "unmanageable." I cried like a baby for nearly half an hour in front of the CEO, the editor in chief, and the senior editor, long-repressed emotions rushing to the surface. In retrospect I realize I was especially wounded that the CEO, a Black man whom I had known for years and for whom I had written at another publication he ran prior to his coming to *Vibe,* was the one who lowered the boom on me as the two White male editors sat and watched. (Yes, he was the CEO, this Black man, but he too had to answer to the White check writer above him. A few years later he would leave, making the same argument I had made: that it was wack to call *Vibe* an urban or Black magazine when the people of color there had no bona fide power, including him.) I felt like I had been professionally lynched for being "an uppity, unappreciative nigga" and that a Black man had participated by throwing the rope over the tree branch. Yes, that is how deeply it cut that it was *he* who spat the lyrics, as unsmiling as a hard-rock MC: "You are fired."

***

FOR SOME REASON—call it my youthful naiveté, call it my stupidity—I was sure I would find employment once more. I did not. I had alienated many, many people during my years at *Vibe*, and some of those individuals were now in a position to decline my job inquiries. One editor said to me, his tone dripping with venom, "I don't have time for superstar writers," and promptly slammed the phone on me. Rejection after rejection led me to believe that I had been whitelisted: *Do not, under any circumstances, have anything to do with Kevin Powell. He is arrogant, unruly, crazy, and prone to temper tantrums.* I was paranoid, thinking folks were taking potshots at me from every bend in the road and that there was an unwritten agreement among industry heads to destroy my writing career. Meanwhile, my wild spending habits had caught up with me. I had no job, no bank account, no rent money. Because my landlord and I were feuding, I was forced to move from my apartment in the heart of the summer, in the middle of this downward spiral. When the world caves in on you, it seems to cave in from every possible direction. I begged my then-girlfriend to permit me to live with her for a few months until I got myself together. Nothing makes a man feel less like a man, if he has any pride whatsoever, than to have to ask his woman to carry him. Totally depressed, there was many a night when I would come home long after my girlfriend had gone to sleep and creep into bed next to her, reeking of liquor, cigar and cigarette smoke, and the perspiration accumulated from combing the streets of New York. How and why my girlfriend tolerated me is beyond me. I would have thrown me out.

I sank further into depression when I realized that I had to sell my massive CD collection, built over a six-year period. Four thousand CDs gone, in three hours of bargaining, for only $1,000. I had no choice, because my wallet was operating on fumes. I also sold my living room set and other items, but gave my bed to a young female poet who needed one. What did I require a bed for when I had no roof to call my own? The next several months were a haze of drinking, a few therapy sessions, more drinking, and the deterioration of my relationship with my girlfriend. She would go off to work, and I would sit at home and gaze at the television, tired, perplexed, and enraged that one magazine editor after another had spurned me or that some editors expected me, after the numerous cover stories I had done at *Vibe*, to begin anew with menial assignments for what I thought was chump change. Had I been that nasty to people? Had I been wrong to protest? Or had it been the *way* I protested? I was absolutely confused and irreconcilably self-doubting. My ideals and identity—the things I was so sure of such a short time before—were all up for grabs. Who was I? As was the case for so many of my generation, my work defined me, and—especially when I was riding a wave of success—I liked it that way. But now it was stripped away, and where did *I* begin? Or was all that I had been now gone, stolen from me by men I didn't even respect? And it was then, right there, that the spidery idea of suicide crawled, on prickly legs, into my mind.

I NEED TO add that being one of the so-called stars of MTV's *The Real World* was the beginning, specifically, of my adult-level bewilderment. I had no clue what I was getting myself into when I was picked, along with six other cast members, to be on the first season of this now legendary TV series. It was a fluke that I had even been "discovered": I was at a 1950s-themed midtown Manhattan restaurant with an R&B band called Joe Public, interviewing them for their record label biography (a way I made a living in those early, happier days), when a smallish White woman approached the table and said she liked our look, then asked if any of us would be interested in interviewing for this new reality-based MTV program. I presumed, unfairly, that the woman was just trying to come on to us Negro studs. But I took the woman's card because my gut told me to do so, thinking that maybe if I wound up on MTV I would subsequently be able to get some college lectures to help pay my bills. I never for the life of me thought that I would become a part of pop culture history, that this would happen in the same year that *Vibe* was inaugurated. I will not lie, either: It was a magical ride—the invite-only, celebrity-riddled parties with an apparently infinite supply of alcohol; the car service whisking me to this interview, to that press conference; the respect I got on the streets in New York City, in Los Angeles, wherever I went in the country, and abroad in London; the money, all the money that came and went buying dinner and drinks for my new "friends" every week as we members of Generation X (isn't that what the "they" who like to advisory-sticker everything young and chic dubbed us?) drowned in the booming economy of the 1990s. It was our sound track, hip-hop—our mission, Andy Warhol's fifteen minutes of fame at any cost and with no shame. Our heroes were Tupac, Bill and Hillary Clinton, the suddenly ubiquitous Sean "Puffy" Combs, millionaire dot-comers, and anyone with the gumption to be their own best logo and boutique business. And our personal credo: Tomorrow is not guaranteed, so live this day like it is your last, baby!

It is sheer lunacy, looking back on it, to have lived like this. It was, indisputably, already an acquiescence to a slow form of suicide, an extended adolescence destined to end in death, not adulthood—a brutally abusive love affair with and fatal attraction to the worst attributes of American culture, American capitalism, American me-ism. But how could I, a little Black boy from the ghetto, have resisted any of that? Heck, how could even a wealthy little White boy from the Upper East Side of Manhattan resist any of that? The carrot on the stick is status, influence, and power—or, more accurately, the fantasies thereof. The difference between the Black boy and the White boy, more times than not, is that the White boy knows—and has been taught religiously, virtually from the cradle—that he can aspire to power on his terms. The Black boy has to erect a fantasy island for himself. That is precisely what I did: I smeared my status in people's faces, so cocksure that others wanted what I had. Nothing wrong with that except I badly overestimated my juice, my power, until it became clear that I had neither because everything I claimed belonged to someone else.

Ergo the survivor's query: What kind of power have we got when we live in a society where our worth is measured by our notoriety and bank accounts, or, in the case of those of us who were mere satellites in this universe, our tenuous connection to those with lots of notoriety and big bank accounts? Too communally insecure to answer this gut-check subpoena, we industry brats rush to the Hamptons; we rush to Martha's Vineyard; we frequent the trendy, exclusive lounges; we squeeze our way into the nouveau riche restaurants where we might run into Leo or Gwyneth or Donald or Martha or Jay-Z or any other first-name-only baller/shot-caller; we drink the latest open-bar concoction (glory be, those apple martinis) from liquor conglomerates eager to reach our demographic; we do not mind being depicted as a marketing scheme, a targeted audience; we bling-bling as if we were rappers in those platinum-studded videos and do not care if we are simply journalists, spoken-word artists, publicists, hair stylists, makeup specialists, models, fashion consultants, DJs, party promoters, or just fans—the most derogatory term of all—along for the ride. For thanks to America's pornographic rapport with all things rubber-stamped "celebrity," we got the feeling (vicarious though it may be) that we are doing big things, nahmean, son? As a consequence, we live these terribly pretentious, plastic lives, runaway *and* runway children, truly, who don't want to grow up, thinking this will go on forever. But was it not the omnipotent, omnipresent Puffy who said the sun don't shine forever?

I could go on, but I bet you get my drift. I was so utterly lost that I did not know who I was, could barely recollect where I came from, rarely called my mother, and dug the fact that when my moms and I did speak she customarily reported that someone from the neighborhood had, once more, seen me on television. Ah, her poor little son, that Black boy with the smile-scowl, had made it to the metaphorical red carpet. It has been said that America eats its young. An addendum: The young will eat themselves if given the proper utensils.

The firing from *Vibe* was a death knell for me. What does one do when the jig is up? Nothing in my life journey had prepared me to climb so high, then be dropped so dramatically low. Life was over, as far as I was concerned, and suicide—the bullet to the head, the poison to the throat, the knife to the wrist—was but a formality. What did I have to lose? Most people don't expect us Black men to live long anyhow. At least I had achieved my childhood dream of being a published writer, right? No regrets. But something nudged me, would never allow me to swallow poison or get a gun and blow my brains away. *There must be,* I reflected on the days I was lucid, *some life lessons here somewhere.*

***

IRONICALLY, I FOUND them when I moved from my girl-friend's apartment to a space, a room, in Harlem. I was pathetically ashamed of my predicament and could not bring myself to seek temporary shelter in the Fort Greene, Brooklyn, 'hood where I had lived large, flossing for the masses to see. I had come full circle, back uptown, back to a room, living hand to mouth, eating at the same hole-in-the-wall soul food and Dominican restaurants as in 1990, when I had had no money. Yes, the human novel lapping itself. This sort of circle confounds the most brilliant among us. At one moment the circle looks like a necessary path; at other times it appears to be a noose dangling above our heads. But in my rented Harlem room I began to find chunks of myself. My landlord was a middle-aged gay Black man, a visual artist, who would come to regard me as a son. I was frightened of life, of people, certain that every-one was fixated on getting at me. I felt like a crackhead who had gone cold turkey without my body's consent. I had been that addicted to the scene, the celebrity, the money. And now I felt undersized, broken, alone, my soul iced and chopped up by a surreal, hazardous lifestyle.

Humanity can be measured in the smallest of acts: the handshake, the smile, the curiosity about another's well-being. When humanity is downgraded to clenched fists, frowns, and a reckless disregard for the person breathing two steps to your left or right, each of us is doomed to an awfully tormented social Darwinism, the individual more important than the community, surviving alone more es-sential than all of us winning in concert. I say this because the man I lived with, who loved to cook, routinely left food for me. Otherwise I would have starved, honestly. He did not know me (I had been recommended by a mutual friend), yet he prepared those plates for me, he loaned me money, he talked with and listened to me. *The men in the Harlem kitchen.* That is how I came to frame our bond as I kick-punched the rock-hard residue of homophobia in my bones and saw this amazing human being, the manliest of men I had come in contact with in a very long time. Who cared what the dude's sexual orientation was? He nurtured me the way my father had not, the way the CEO who fired me ultimately did not (I fought him for several months to get a minuscule severance package). And this man, this gay Black man, taught me more lessons about manhood than one would think possible: that one could be a man, be responsible, be kind, be loving, show love, give love, without compromising one's self-worth and dignity. The source of his power—and he was powerful—was in his own simple humanity, his wholly self-possessed life. He taught me, just by being who he was, that without knowing what I was doing I had leveraged my manhood—no, my humanity— to forces and individuals that not only were beyond my control but were openly hostile to my survival. He did not know me from a can of paint, but he, this man, did these things for me.

I had been guilty of verbally bashing, privately and publicly, men with his sexual orientation as "fags" or "homos." This chance encounter began a reassessment, in another stratosphere, of what it is to be a man, and by whose definitions. I had been among the armies of straight fellas who routinely justify our power(lessness) by dehumanizing men we perceive to be weak or soft. It was me, indeed, who had been weak and soft from the jump, my fragile existence glued in place by the superficiality of my dependence on fame, money, and unmitigated pleasure. As I lay on my thin mattress in the African darkness of Harlem I would fix my eyes on the ceiling, wondering how I had lost myself so easily to the temptations of the material world. And I would shed buckets of tears some nights as the shrieks, the screams, and gun blasts of Harlem hovered outside my window like the death stench from a gas chamber. I felt imprisoned by a past I had long sought to escape. Perhaps, I reckoned, this is a reminder that no matter where you go, you can never escape where you come from. That time humbled me in a way I had never been humbled in my entire life. Things that had previously meant a great deal to me—the magnetic trinkets of the entertainment industry—were suddenly meaningless.

I didn't write for a lengthy stretch, and when I finally did—a free article for a college Internet news service—it was as special as my first high-paying piece for a national magazine. And I have been writing and living, fully, since. I now reside in my own apartment, back in Brooklyn, enjoying the unfussy delights of life, like Yankee Stadium, an old movie, a Marvin Gaye song, a Keats poem. I no longer take anything for granted. People often ask, "What are you doing now?" and I beam and respond, "Just living, yo." I stopped drinking altogether when a holistic doctor told me the course I was on would lead to a badly contaminated liver. While I don't believe I was an alcoholic, I do believe I could have become one. My depression and ballooning self-hatred were entrenched in my spirit, for sure. Nowadays I try to respect myself and other people, although I have slipped on more than a few occasions. The demons are going to be there, on your shoulder, whispering in your ear. I am still very concerned about injustices and still insist I was right about the lack of Black editors and the power struggles at *Vibe*. But the bigger lesson I gleaned from that entire crazy episode is that success defined in a material way means nothing if you are not successful at negotiating the unpredictable terrain of life and if you don't really know yourself. I will, without fail, argue that racism coupled with my unflinching working-class perspective and my bad-boy persona were major factors contributing to my downfall. Yes, each of those things did play a significant role. But the true measure of any human being, I have come to believe, is your ability to take some personal responsibility to reverse the crack-up, the breakdown, and not be afraid to stop the cycles of self-pity, sit alone in the quiet of your own room, and stitch yourself back together. Because that self you repair is the only thing that's truly yours, the ultimate source of true power. I pray that I never sink to that point again, where life and love—particularly self-love—seem utterly useless and disposable. And I have never wanted to live and love as badly as I do right now.

CONFESSIONS
OF A

RECOVERING
MISOGYNIST

I am a sexist male.

TAKE NO GREAT PRIDE IN SAYING THIS. I AM MERELY stating a fact. It is not that I was born this way; rather, I was born into this male-dominated society, and, consequently, from the very moment I began forming thoughts, they formed in a decidedly male-centered way. My "education" at home with my mother, at school, on my neighborhood playgrounds, and at church all placed males at the center of the universe. My digestion of 1970s American popular culture in the form of television, film, ads, and music only added to my training, so that by as early as age nine or ten I saw females, including my mother, as nothing more than the servants of males. Indeed, like the Fonz on that TV sitcom *Happy Days*, I thought I could snap my fingers and girls would come running.

My mother, working poor and a product of the conservative and patriarchal South, simply raised me as most women are taught to raise boys: The world was mine, there were no chores to speak of, and my aggressions were considered somewhat normal, something that we boys carry out as a rite of passage. Those "rites" included me routinely squeezing girls' butts on the playground. And at school boys were encouraged to do "boy" things: work and build with our hands, fight each other, and participate in the most daring activities during our gym time. Meanwhile, the girls were relegated to home economics, drawing cute pictures, and singing in the school choir. Now that I think about it, school was the place that spearheaded the omission of women from my worldview. Save Betsy Ross (whom I remember chiefly for sewing a flag) and a stoic Rosa Parks (she was unfurled every year as an example of Black achievement), I recall virtually no women making appearances in my American history classes.

THE CHURCH MY mother and I attended, like most Black churches, was peopled mainly by Black women, most of them single parents, who dragged their children along for the ride. Not once did I see a preacher who was anything other than an articulate, emotionally charged, well-coiffed, impeccably suited Black man running this church and, truly, these women. And behind the pulpit of this Black man, where he convinced us we were doomed to hell if we did not get right with God, was the image of our savior, a male, always White, named Jesus Christ.

Not surprisingly, the "savior" I wanted in my life was my father. Ten years her senior, my father met my mother, my father wooed my mother, my father impregnated my mother, and then my father—as per *his* socialization—

moved on to the next mating call. Responsibility was about as real to him as a three-dollar bill. When I was eight, my father flatly told my mother, via a pay phone, that he felt she had lied, that I was not his child, and that he would never give her money for me again. The one remotely tangible image of maleness in my life was gone for good. Both my mother and I were devastated, albeit for different reasons. I longed for my father's affections. And my mother longed to be married. Silently I began to blame my mother for my father's disappearance. Reacting to my increasingly bad behavior, my mother turned resentful and her beatings became more frequent, more charged. I grew to hate her and all females, for I felt it was women who made men act as we do.

At the same time, my mother, a fiercely independent and outspoken woman despite having only a grade-school education and being poor, planted within me the seeds of self-criticism, of shame for wrongful behavior—and, ultimately, of feminism. Clear that she alone would have to shape me, my mother spoke pointedly about my father for many years after that call, demanding that I not grow up to "be like him." And I noted the number of times my mother rejected low-life male suitors, particularly the ones who wanted to live with us free of charge. I can see now that my mother is a feminist, although she is not readily familiar with the term. Like many women before and since, she fell hard for my father, and only through enduring immense pain did she realize the power she had within herself.

I once hated women, and I take no pride in this confession.

I entered Rutgers University in the mid-1980s, and my mama's-boy demeanor advanced to that of pimp. I learned quickly that most males in college are some variety of pimp. Today I lecture regularly, from campus to campus, all over the country, and I see that not much has changed. For college is simply a place where we men, irrespective of race or class, can—and do—act out the sexist attitudes entrenched since boyhood. Rape, infidelity, girlfriend beatdowns, and emotional abuse are common, and pimpdom reigns supreme. There is the athlete pimp, the frat boy pimp, the independent pimp, and the college professor pimp. Buoyed by the antiapartheid movement and the presidential bids of Jesse Jackson, my social consciousness blossomed along racial lines, and behold—the student leader pimp was born.

Blessed with a gift for gab, a poet's sensibility, and an acute memory for historical facts, I baited women with my self-righteousness by quoting Malcolm X, Frantz Fanon, Machiavelli, and any other figure I was sure they had not studied. It was a polite form of sexism, for I was always certain to say "my sister" when I addressed women at Rutgers. But my politeness did not lend me tolerance for women's issues, nor did my affiliation with a variety of Black nationalist organizations, especially the Nation of Islam. Indeed, whenever women in our African Student Congress would question the behavior and attitudes of men, I would scream, "We don't have time for them damn lesbian issues!" My scream was violent, mean-spirited, made with the intention to wound. I don't think it is any coincidence that during my four years in college I did not have one relationship with a woman that lasted more than three or four months. For every friend or girlfriend who would dare question my deeds, there were literally hundreds of others who acquiesced to the ways of us men, making it easy for me to ignore the legitimate cries of the feminists. Besides, I had taken on the demanding role of pimp, of conqueror, of campus revolutionary—there was little time or room for real intimacy, and even less time for self-reflection.

Confessions are difficult because they force me to visit ghettos in the mind I thought I had long escaped.

I was kicked out of college at the end of my fourth year because I drew a knife on a female student. We were both members of the African Student Congress, and she was one of the many "subversive" female leaders I had sought to purge from the organization. She *had* left but for some reason was in our office a few days after we had brought Louis Farrakhan to speak at Rutgers. Made tense by her presence, I ignored her and turned to a male student, asking him, as she stood there, to ask her to jet. As she was leaving, she turned and charged toward me. My instincts, nurtured by my inner-city upbringing and several months of receiving anonymous threats as the Farrakhan talk neared, caused me to reach into my pocket and pull out a knife I had been carrying.

My intent was to scare her into submission. The male student panicked and knocked the knife from my hand, believing I was going to stab this woman. I would like to believe that that was not the case. It did not matter. This woman pressed charges on and off campus, and my college career, the one I'd taken on for myself, my undereducated mother, and my illiterate grandparents, came to a screeching halt.

It is not easy for me to admit I have a problem.

Before I could be readmitted to school I had to see a therapist. I went, grudgingly, and agonized over my violent childhood, my hatred of my mother, my many problems with women, and the nauseating torment of poverty and instability. But then it was done. I did not bother to try to return to college, and I found myself again using women for money, for sex, for entertainment. When I moved to New York City in August 1990, my predator mentality was still in full effect. I met a woman, persuaded her to allow me to live with her, and then mentally abused her for nearly a year, cutting her off from some of her friends, shredding her peace of mind and her spirit. Eventually I pushed her into the bathroom door when she blew up my spot, challenging me and my manhood.

I do not want to recount the details of the incident here. What I will say is that I, like most Black men I know, have spent much of my life living in fear: fear of White racism, fear of the circumstances that gave birth to me, fear of walking out my door wondering what humiliation will be mine today. Fear of Black women—of their mouths, of their bodies, of their attitudes, of their hurts, of their fear of us Black men. I felt fragile, as fragile as a bird with clipped wings, that day when my ex-girlfriend stepped up her game and spoke back to me. Nothing in my world, nothing in my self-definition prepared me for dealing with a woman as an equal. My world said women were inferior, that they must at all costs be put in their place, and my instant reaction was to do that. When it was over, I found myself dripping with sweat, staring at her back as she ran barefoot out of the apartment.

Guilt consumed me after the incident. The women I knew through my circle of poet and writer friends begged me to talk through what I had done, to get counseling, to read the books of bell hooks, Pearl Cleage's tiny tome *Mad at Miles*, the poetry of Audre Lorde, the many meditations of Gloria Steinem. I resisted at first, but eventually I began to listen and read, feeling electric shocks running through my body when I realized that these women, in describing abusive, oppressive men, were talking about me. Me, who thought I was progressive. Me, who claimed to be a leader. Me, who still felt women were on the planet to take care of men.

During this time I did restart therapy sessions. I also

spent a good deal of time talking with young feminist women—some friends, some not. Some were soothing and understanding, some berated me and all men. I also spent a great deal of time alone, replaying my life in my mind: my relationship with my mother, how my mother had responded to my father's actions, how I had responded to my mother's response to my father. I thought of my education, of the absence of women in it. How I'd managed to attend a major university affiliated with one of the oldest women's colleges in America, Douglass College, and visited that campus only in pursuit of sex. I thought of the older men I had encountered in my life—the ministers, the high school track coach, the street hustlers, the local businessmen, the college professors, the political and community leaders— and realized that many of the ways I learned to relate to women came from listening to and observing those men. Yeah, I grew up after women's studies classes had appeared in most of the colleges in America, but that doesn't mean feminism actually reached the people it really needed to reach: average, everyday American males.

The incident, and the remorse that followed, brought about something akin to a spiritual epiphany. I struggled mightily to rethink the context that had created my mother. And my aunts. And my grandmother. And all the women I had been intimate with, either physically or emotionally or both. I struggled to understand terms like *patriarchy, misogyny, gender oppression.* A year after the incident I penned a short essay for *Essence* magazine called, simply, "The Sexist in Me," because I wanted to be honest in the most public forum possible, and because I wanted to reach some men, some young Black men, who needed to hear from another male that sexism is as oppressive as racism. And at times worse.

I am no hero. I am no saint. I remain a sexist male.

But one who is now conscious of it and who has been waging an internal war for several years. Some days I am incredibly progressive; other days I regress. It is very lonesome to swim against the stream of American male-centeredness, of Black male bravado and nut grabbing. It is how I was molded, it is what I know, and in rejecting it I often feel mad naked and isolated. For example, when I publicly opposed the blatantly sexist and patriarchal rhetoric and atmosphere of the Million Man March, I was attacked by Black men, some questioning my sanity, some accusing me of being a dupe for the White man, and some wondering if I was just "tryin' to get some pussy from Black women."

Likewise, I am a hip-hop head. Since adolescence I have been involved in this culture, this lifestyle, as a dancer, a graffiti writer, an activist, a concert organizer, and most prominently a hip-hop journalist. Indeed, as a reporter at *Vibe* magazine, I found myself interviewing rap icons like Dr. Dre, Snoop Dogg, and the late Tupac Shakur. And although I did ask Snoop and Tupac some pointed questions about *their* sexism, I still feel I dropped the ball. We Black men often feel so powerless, so sure the world—politically, economically, spiritually, and psychologically—is aligned against us. The last thing any of us wants is for another man to question how we treat women. Aren't we, Black men, the endangered species anyhow? This is how many of us think.

While I do not think hip-hop is any more sexist or misogynist than other forms of American culture, I do think it is the most explicit form of misogyny around today. It is also a form of sexism that gets more than its share of attention, because hip-hop—now a billion-dollar industry—is the sound track for young America, regardless of race or class. What folks don't understand is that hip-hop was created on the heels of the Civil Rights era by impoverished Blacks and Latinos, who literally made something out of nothing. But in making that something out of nothing, many of us men of color have held tightly to White patriarchal notions of manhood—that is, the way to be a man is to have power. Within hip-hop culture, in our lyrics, in our videos, and on our tours, that power translates into material possessions, provocative and often foul language, flashes of violence, and blatant objectification of and disrespect for women. Patriarchy, as manifested in hip-hop, is where we can have our version of power within this very oppressive society. Who would want to even consider giving that up?

Well, I have, to a large extent, and these days I am a hip-hopper in exile. I dress, talk, and walk like a hip-hopper, yet I cannot listen to rap radio or digest music videos without commenting on the pervasive sexism. Moreover, I try to drop seeds, as we say, about sexism, whenever and wherever I can, be it at a community forum or on a college campus. Some men, young and old alike, simply cannot deal with it and walk out. Or there is the nervous shifting in seats, the uneasy comments during the question-and-answer sessions, generally in the form of "Why you gotta pick on the men, man?" I constantly "pick on the men" and myself because I truly wonder how many men actually listen to the concerns of women. Just as I feel it is Whites who need to be more vociferous about racism in their communities, I feel it is men who need to speak long and loud about sexism among ourselves.

I am a recovering misogynist.

I do not say this with pride. Like a recovering alcoholic or a crack fiend who has righted her or his ways, I am merely cognizant of the fact that I have had some serious problems in my life with and in regard to women. I am also aware of the fact that I can lapse at any time. My relationship with my mother is better than it has ever been, though there are days when speaking with her turns me back into that little boy cowering beneath the belt and tongue of a woman deeply wounded by my father, by poverty, by her childhood, by the sexism that has dominated her life. My relationships since the incident with my ex-girlfriend have been better, no doubt, but not the bomb.

But I am at least proud of the fact I have not reverted back to violence against women—and don't ever plan to, which is why I regularly go to therapy, why I listen to and absorb the stories of women, and why I talk about sexism with any men, young and old, who are down to rethink the definitions we've accepted so uncritically. Few of us men actually believe there is a problem, or we are quick to point fingers at women, instead of acknowledging that healing is a necessary and ongoing process, that women *and* men need to be a part of this process, and that we all must be willing to engage in this dialogue and work if sexism is to ever disappear.

So I fly solo, and have done so for some time. For sure, today I count among my friends, peers, and mentors older feminist women like bell hooks and Johnnetta B. Cole, and young feminists like Nikki Stewart, a girls' rights advocate in Washington, D.C., and Aishah Simmons, who is currently putting together a documentary on rape within the Black community. I do not always agree with these women, but I also know that if I do not struggle, hard and constantly, backsliding is likely. This is made worse by the fact that outside of a handful of male friends, there are no young men I know whom I can speak with regarding sexism as easily as I do with women.

The fact is, there was a blueprint handed to us in childhood telling us this is the way a man should behave, and we unwittingly followed the script verbatim. There was no blueprint handed to us about how to begin to wind ourselves out of sexism as an adult, but maybe there should have been. Every day I struggle within myself not to use the language of gender oppression, to see the sexism inherent in every aspect of America, to challenge all injustices, not just those that are convenient for me. I am ashamed of my ridiculously sexist life, of raising my hand to my girlfriend, and of two other ugly and hateful moments in college, one where I hit a female student in the head with a stapler during the course of an argument, and the other where I got into a punch-throwing exchange with a female student I had sexed then discarded like an old pair of shoes. I am also ashamed of all the lies and manipulations, the verbal abuse and reckless disregard for the views and lives of women. But with that shame has come a consciousness and, as the activists said during the Civil Rights Movement, this consciousness, this knowing, is a river of no return. I have finally learned how to swim. I have finally learned how to push forward. I may become tired, I may lose my breath, I may hit a rock from time to time and become cynical, but I am not going to drown this time around.

WHAT IS A

MAN?

no you won't be name'n no buildings
after me
to go down dilapidated

      —Erykah Badu, "A.D. 2000"

Moral courage is a rarer commodity than
bravery in battle or great intelligence.

      —Robert F. Kennedy,
      "A Tiny Ripple of Hope"

PART I

THE DEATH OF A HUMAN BEING, PARTICULARLY A human being one has come to know fairly well on one level or another, has a funny way of making one realize, in a hurry, one's own mortality and limitations. The presence of death remains, whether we care to admit it or not, one last and halting breath away, every day of our lives. I personally have had, since I was a very bad and very foul-mouthed little Black boy, an extremely ambiguous relationship with death. I just never got it. Uh-huh, sure, the churches I attended offered the clichéd, knee-jerk interpretation: Live a good life and you shall get to heaven; live a life of sin and you shall bust hell wide open. But the threat of eternal damnation had a surprisingly light hold on me. On those days I had off from da Lawd, I wondered what hell could be worse than the ghetto life to which I was born. But even as some of us whistle past the grave-yard, dreaming our visions of life after life, the perplexing truth is that we have no idea what's out there for us after we're gone, nor do we have any control over when, as the old folks down South like to say, it's your time. If you happen to be poor and young and Black and male and confronted by death at every corner you turn, sooner or later you stop wondering when you're going to go and start thinking about *how* you are going to go. If you grew up the way a lot of us did—in the blood-soaked '70s, '80s, and '90s, when murder rates for young black men around the country climbed into the domain of battlefield casualties—you may have been quickly and altogether rationally convinced that it was only a matter of time before the grim reaper stepped. Which is why, as bizarre as it seems, it's really not all that surprising that in inner cities across America at this hour young Black men, especially those who have access to long paper (ya know the deal: the not-so-holy trinity of drug dealers, rappers, and ballplayers), are going to local funeral parlors and paying for their own coffins and funerals in advance of their anticipated deaths. Some heads actually purchase coffins to match the style and make of their late-model cars or sport utility vehicles. Yes, I have seen this with my own eyes, and yes, excessive materialism knows no boundaries, not even the unexplorable frontier of death, and yes, life expectations are simply that low.

Which brings me to the late Tupac Amaru Shakur. To be brutally honest, over seven years have passed and I still feel I have not properly mourned Tupac's horribly tragic end. I don't know if it is because I had been expecting his death for so long before it arrived, or if I have simply become numb to the death marches of Black men. Or perhaps it is because I linger in denial, thinking that Tupac, like the Yoruba deity Shango, is such a regal spirit, such a warrior, such a master of the drum, the dance, and the oration that he will live forever. Like everybody else, I don't want to believe that death is more certain than life, although all experience tells us it *is*. What I have also done during this time is think long and hard about the vulnerable Black boys and men who are still around and, like their patron saint Shakur, walking time bombs. And about the wicked trajectory of my own life. And about the lives of the hundreds and thousands of Black men who have crossed my path as far back as I can remember. For some reason, thinking about the lives of these men, these boys, always brings me back to 'Pac.

I've absorbed a plethora of books, statistics, commissioned reports, documentaries, press clippings, and one-on-one and group conversations, each in its own way staking a claim of relevance to the real estate known as the state of the Black man circa the present. No matter the forum, the questions I keep coming back to are the same: *Who am I? Who are we?* The first question is crucial because, logically, how can I seriously begin to account for someone else's life, like Tupac Shakur's, if I can barely account for my own? Yet I learned a long time ago that in accounting for my own life, I have to account for the lives of other Black men. We are, after all, connected by the hard sinew of race, gender, and culture, booked for common passage on that beleaguered battleship christened history. Consequently, without sounding delusional or arrogant, the questions of who I am and who we are are actually closely connected in a historical sense, even as the answers diverge a million ways based on our individual choices and experiences.

This is what led me to Tupac Shakur in the first place. When I signed on as a staff writer at *Vibe* magazine in the spring of 1993, I was asked to think about subjects I thought would be of interest to our burgeoning "urban" readership. When Tupac Shakur made his motion picture debut in Ernest Dickerson's film *Juice* in the winter of 1992, a lot of heads—including me—walked into the theater not knowing what to expect, unaware of what we were about to witness. In the film, Tupac was a two-headed young Harlemite named Bishop who, along with his three partners in crime, cut school, played arcade games at the corner store, and inadvertently courted beef with the neighborhood thugs. I remember my trip to see the film when it first opened. Back then I was living in uptown Manhattan and was with my friend and fellow poet Tony Medina, heading to the theater on 145th and Broadway, where Harlem meets the Dominican Republic. We rolled up to the movie theater excitedly, only to be confronted with metal detectors, police barricades, and a couple of officers milling about, one with a German shepherd on a leash. In the two years after movies like *New Jack City* and *Boyz 'N the Hood* came out and found commercial success, Hollywood was—for a hot minute—hooked on stories of new Black male angst. The flip side was that the release of each 'hood film seemed to be accompanied by a violent disruption at a theater somewhere in America. The expectations for *Juice* were no different, hence the tight security measures. From what I can recall, the theater was nearly empty, but the screen was filled with the enormous, commanding presence of Tupac Shakur. I watched this brother walk with ease through his role, fully inhabiting his character, making an effortless transition from the fun-loving homie at the beginning of the movie to the quick-tempered murderer who ended it. There was *something* about Tupac or Bishop or whoever that was up on the screen. With his voice and his body and the sudden flash of his eyes, Tupac had the rare ability to convey both the beauty and the ugliness of contemporary young Black manhood, its fearlessness and braggadocio and bottomless yearning. With that single performance, Tupac captured the complexities of 1990s Black male inner turmoil much in the way Marlon Brando or James Dean had captured young White male bewilderment and desperation in the 1950s. As the drama unfolded in the darkness of the theater I watched Bishop up on-screen but thought about Tupac Shakur: about his brief membership in the Oakland-based hip-hop group Digital Underground, about his solo career, and about those eyes of his—how dark and wide and alert they were, how they seemed to belong to another place, another era, some royal order.

It wasn't like I was sweating Tupac or anything like that. It was just mad cool to see a young Black man I could relate to in a popular medium. Will "Fresh Prince" Smith was a little too corny, Kadeem Hardison was a little too

75

nice, and rappers like KRS-One and Ice Cube were instantly important but had limitations—some personal, some political—that kept a lid on their mass appeal. On the other hand, Tupac, beginning in full force when he made that star turn in *Juice,* became the poster boy for ghetto bastards everywhere. He was a young rebel without a pause on an uncompromising mission to leave his stain on a world that he was convinced had rejected him. But the world that mattered most to Tupac, the ghettos of America, embraced him. He would tell me later, proudly, that after appearing in *Juice* he could walk into any Black community in America and "get love and respect from niggas." To understand how Black manhood functions in the ghetto is to know, positively, that respect is the only currency that matters, the true taste of power. Without respect you have nothing and are regarded as less than nothing.

After leaving the movie theater, I knew that I had to write a profile on Tupac Shakur. At the time Nirvana's Kurt Cobain was considered the voice of alienated White youth, and I thought it was important that my community identify the artists who spoke to our disaffection. For the next few months I collected Tupac's music videos, taped his television and radio interviews, and saved every article I could find. I also began collecting informal oral histories from folks who either knew Tupac or had encountered him in some way. The first stories that came in became the building blocks of what would develop into the full-blown myth of Tupac: on tour, Tupac, defender of women, had protected rapper Queen Latifah from a disrespectful young man. Tupac, hot-tempered revolutionary, had beaten down a brother who dared steal something from rap's reigning black superheroes, Public Enemy. Tupac, ghetto bastard, didn't know who his own father was. Tupac, gifted prodigy, had attended the highly regarded Baltimore School of the Arts and excelled as a student-actor. Tupac, protean polymath, loved Shakespeare and classical music but had a chameleon's capacity to transform himself completely from one moment to the next. And Tupac, for whom geography would eventually become destiny, never had a stable home; born in New York City, he and his family moved a great deal, around New York City, to Baltimore, and finally to Marin City in northern California. The stories were endless, layered, and intriguing. And I was hooked.

In September 1993, several months after the premiere of *Juice*, my editors gave me the go-ahead to do a feature article on Tupac. I had met Tupac for the first time a month before, in Atlanta at the Black music industry's then annual "Jack the Rapper" conference. He was surprisingly taller and leaner than I anticipated, and was then fresh off his starring role opposite Janet Jackson in John Singleton's bland ghetto love story, *Poetic Justice*. But even as the movie produced yawns, Tupac, as had been the case with *Juice*, received the best reviews. I wasn't quite sure how to approach him, so I just stood to the side with Karla Radford, my good friend and *Vibe*'s special-events director, and watched Tupac check into the hotel. I observed a number of women—fine women—ooh and aah in his direction. Karla knew it was important for me to meet Tupac, and she walked over to him and told him so. I was red-faced, but to my surprise Tupac turned in my direction and instantly recognized me from MTV's *The Real World* (I had been a cast member during its inaugural season).

"Whassup dogg! I had your back on that show, man! You told them White folks what the real deal was. . . ."

Tupac went on and on like a little kid. That was the first disconcerting, but disarming, aspect of him: He was not quite a man but also not a little boy. He was somewhere in between. Here I was nervous about meeting him, and he had as much respect for me as I had for him. I told Tupac that I wanted to do a major piece on him, and he was excited about the idea. Tupac told me to call his then manager, Watani, to set things up. I was mad open because I felt that an article on Tupac, even more so than the *Vibe* features I had already done on Treach of Naughty by Nature and Snoop Dogg, was going to be a definitive piece on what it meant to be a young Black male in post–civil rights America. I even had some titles in my head for the piece. One was "Portrait of the Artist as a Young Black Male." Yup, mad corny. But I did not care back then, because something way down in my gut told me that this article and this connection with Tupac was going to be *big*. Little did I know that this initial meeting would be the beginning of a long and difficult journey with Tupac Shakur, one that would challenge me both as a writer and as a man.

Without a doubt, it was ridiculously surreal and seductive, especially as I reflect upon that rite of passage now. I instantly felt a deep kinship with Tupac, but I knew I wasn't alone. Tupac represented the journey of his generation writ large and damned dramatic, right from his beginning, when his mother carried him in her belly while locked behind bars, incarcerated as a member of the Black Panther Party. I had been a student activist at Rutgers University and after college had worked in community-based activist organizations, and I had a strong affinity for that aspect of our history, the stories of activists and revolutionaries. Tupac Shakur, I believed, was the direct link, the bridge, that the civil rights and hip-hop generations so badly needed. I became more convinced of this when during an interview Afeni Shakur, Tupac's mother, told me, "I never thought Tupac would make it here alive" because while she was pregnant and in prison she had to survive on "one egg and one glass of milk per day" for herself and her unborn son. This was the centerpiece of the Tupac mythology, the piece that affirmed to me that Tupac was special, destined from the moment he was born on June 16, 1971, in New York City, to leave a dent on his generation and on this world. Afeni Shakur knew this before me, believing it even at his birth. She saw him as a wonder boy, the miracle survivor, her warrior, and she dug into the cultural crates and crowned him Tupac Amaru Shakur. Tupac was named after an Inca chief: *Tupac Amaru* means "shining serpent," referring to wisdom and courage. *Shakur* is Arabic for "thankful to God." The name was a sign of those times, when Black folks were getting rid of their "slave names" and taking on handles that implied something African, something political, something relevant to their newly discovered Black lives. LeRoi Jones became Amiri Baraka. Don L. Lee became Haki Madhubuti. And so on. That generation was determined to break the mental shackles of the past. *Shakur* was also the surname of many prominent members of the Black liberation movement—the early 1970s urban-based and radical offshoot of the civil rights battles—with the legendary prison escapee Assata Shakur being one of the more famous bearers of that politically charged moniker. Moreover, given that this young man's astrological sign was Gemini, we know he had two sides warring with each other: good and evil, kindness and mean-spiritedness, love and hate, war and peace, African and American, scholar and class clown, revolutionary and thug for life. So, I thought then, to discuss Tupac Shakur was to discuss the state of Black manhood and the state of Black America—the era of Black America he was born into and the one that he helped define. More so than any rapper in hip-hop history up to that point (or even after), Tupac poignantly captured the totality of the contemporary Black male experience.

Thus Tupac could never be one thing or one person for too long—that was simply not his nature, nor his style. I peeped this the first time I listened to his 1991 debut album, *2Pacalypse Now.* Tupac was not, in my mind, a great rapper. In terms of pure mic skills he would never make my top five list of great MCs of all time—not if the ranking had to do with organic mic capabilities. His gruff baritone was never on a par with the creative vocal geniuses of hip-hop: KRS-One, Snoop Dogg, Rakim, Ice Cube, Big Daddy Kane, Scarface, Chuck D., or Andre from the group Outkast. Not even close. He was, let us say, a good-enough rapper who had *great* moments during the course of his oh-so-short but amazingly prolific career. More than with his voice, he seduced fans in the video era with his stunningly handsome features: the high, jagged cheek-bones, the thick, bushy eyebrows, the sleepy, almond-shaped eyes, the long, girlish eyelashes, and the radiant, toothy smile. His great musical moments were teamed with movie star magnetism, uncontrollable passion, and boyish charm. And his lyrics, delivered with a fistful of machine-gun machismo, expressed his deeply rooted social consciousness, a violent distaste for injustice, an intellect that devoured everything from street-corner polemics to the ruminations of Machiavelli, and, more than anything, an unshakable loyalty to family, fans, friends, Black people, and humanity. Tupac was the one who wouldn't sell you out. Those intangibles are what made Tupac Shakur (or 2Pac, as it was spelled for the hip-hop nation) the most compelling voice of his generation. Put another way, Tupac had an uncanny ability to move easily across the fractured landscape of hip-hop, from the Black nationalistic rhetoric of Public Enemy to the harsh ghetto oratory of N.W.A. to the playfulness of his homeboys in Digital Underground and all points in between. On that very first album, Tupac Shakur proclaimed that he was not going to be locked in by anyone's definition of what a Black man was or should be. It made no difference if you or I agreed or disagreed with Tupac. Nor did he care. What was imperative, as far as he was concerned, was that he had finally found a voice, his voice.

Tupac had fans across the American demographic—including that much-discussed majority of White hip-hop fans. But in order to process what it was to be Tupac Shakur, it's not enough to listen to his music; you have to first understand what it was like for him to grow up with poverty and pain as the cornerstones on which his life was being erected. I felt I knew this aspect of the man Tupac the moment I first heard one of 'Pac's breakthrough hits, the bleak urban tragedy "Brenda's Got a Baby." I knew because the world Tupac was born into, I was born into. Ghetto children can immediately sense the steely presence of our comrades. It is in the pitch of the voice, the hock-spit that whisks around the base of the throat, the drab isolation shadowing the eyes, the sugar-filled energy threading its way through our loping strides. To be a Black boy turned out by the horrific conditions of America's gutters is to be a Black boy fighting for survival every minute of your life. I say this not to sound sensational or provocative or self-pitying. It is merely a fact. Visit any hard-core Black community in America in this new millennium—I dare you—and note how many Black boys and Black men do not feel tomorrow is ever going to come. I heard Tupac's reality in his words and the breath that gave them life. I heard my own story between the lines. I knew Tupac did not know his father because I had not known my father. I knew Tupac was mad hungry many days because I had been mad hungry many days. I knew Tupac was hemmed in by anger, disorientation, fear, and bitterness because I too did a jig with anger, disorientation, fear, and bitterness. I knew Tupac loved and hated his mother because I both loved and hated my mother. We Black boys and Black men may often fight each other because we do not know whom we really should be fighting, but at root we are kindred spirits.

THE KINSHIP THAT ultimately formed the connection between Tupac and the Black men who made him their hero is rooted in the first definitively American experience: slavery. I can hear the dubious among you right this minute: *I thought this story was about beats and rhymes and self-destruction, about Tupac. Why is he bringing up slavery?* That's precisely why I'm bringing it up—because the story of Tupac, the story of the Black-power culture that birthed him and the hip-hop culture that gave him a reason for being, is only the latest chapter of a story that began in slavery. To understand Tupac—to understand Black *and* White manhood—we got to go back. I bring it up because America has never fully dealt with the effects of that peculiar institution upon both slave and slave master.

All of us were affected, profoundly, and what a way to have one's manhood defined: Either you are supreme captain of the universe, ruler of everything you can fit beneath your pale, fat thumb, or you are a dark, strapping buck, a sexual stud, a dim-witted sloth or grinning minstrel, or some combination thereof, unable to function without the direction and nudges (ah, yes, the whip) of the master. And slavery, for all its horrors, was just the beginning. Between the time *physical* slavery ended in America (1865) and the time the Civil Rights Movement was jump-started (the mid-1950s) more Black men than we would like to think about found themselves chased from towns, burned alive, hung from trees, and on more than a few occasions castrated. *Castrated.* If you were one of the Scottsboro boys in the 1930s, being in the wrong place at the wrong time meant you could be accused of raping White women and presumed guilty before a trial, without any hard evidence, just because you were a nigga. Imagine having your manhood classified by—no, predicated on—how White males or White females in your particular town or city or region or state felt on any given day. On a good day you might merely be called "boy" or "nigga" or "coon." On a bad day, you could end up swinging from a rope. If that kind of cruel uncertainty doesn't result in a suffocating form of paranoid schizophrenia—as natural to one's essence as the color of one's skin—then I don't know what would. And as I have said on many occasions in my public lectures, Black people in America have never—*never*—had a mass therapy session to deal with the devastating consequences of slavery and its aftermath: legalized segregation and second-class citizenship. What did all of that do to our minds, to our bodies, to our souls? When did we ever pause to flip the pages of our collective mental photo album and reflect, grimace, laugh, cry, scream? What did it do to Black women, to Black men, to the relations between Black women and men? What parts of that experience became integrated into the DNA of our culture, as much a part of our "traditions" as eating fried chicken, drinking sweetened iced tea, or stirring up Christianity with that spiritual gumbo we call "roots" or "superstitions"? To interpolate that Louis Armstrong couplet: What did we do to become Black and so goddamn blue? Has there ever been any time, any spare room, for us to *process* any of this? To separate the blues from straight-up depression and psychosis? "Keep this nigger-boy running," Ellison wrote in *Invisible Man*. Yep, running in place—or backward.

When I hear folks who are Jewish say, "Never forget," I understand that they mean the Holocaust was so devastating to their people in its intentional, systematic destructiveness that they must make sure the healing process is ongoing, passed like a baton in a relay race from one family member to the next, from this generation to that one. The process of perpetual remembrance is so thorough that it permeates their culture, their (self-)education, their art, their literature, and, in a fundamental way, how they navigate their way through this world as a people. I ain't mad at them, either. They do what they gotta to make sure that madness don't never happen again.

Colored people at the end of the first phase of their Holocaust were simply told they were free and released to an uncertain future. A few got some land and some education and some money, but most did not and remained economic slaves, sharecropping, tenant-farming, playing Uncle

Tom and Aunt Jemina, or otherwise hustling to remain alive. And colored people have had to lug around the added burden of being marked as a minority, defined by the dominant culture as the "other," the outsider whose purpose is to reflect or define White life, usually in the negative, to function as an antithesis of the ideal. To the degree that Black life was examined, it was in the vocabulary of pathology. The White man's burden . . . the Negro problem . . . the conundrum of race . . . and so on. I am not into comparing oppressions, but the reality is that what people of African descent have had to endure on these shores dates back about five hundred years. Five long, difficult centuries. Half a millennium. Save the slaughter of Native Americans, no group has had to endure so much and for so long in this house we call America. And unless you were one of the minority of the numerical minority fortunate enough to be blessed with privilege—education, money, the ability to eat on a daily basis—your existence and wretchedness essentially were, and are, twins discharged from the same oppressive womb, your life's possibilities reduced to what could be manufactured from that patch of land, that crack in the concrete, inside that shack, inside that tenement or project. What a place to find a definition for yourself: inside a box given to you by someone else. Chill in that box long enough and risk having your back bent permanently, like a question mark. Dare to rise from that box and death lurks, itching to club you upside the head. From the box we come and to the box we return.

The collective Black male experience, from the end of slavery until the middle of the last century, revolved mainly around accommodating Mister Charlie and Miss Ann, or telling Mister Charlie and Miss Ann to kiss where the sun don't shine. With either option, some mode of death was assured and the polestar of Black identity remained Whiteness. But then something began to change in the mid-1950s. Maybe it was the aftermath of World War II and the return of Black soldiers who had fought for freedom abroad and sought it on their native soil. Maybe it was a shared weariness with accepting business as usual. And maybe, just maybe, there was a surging feeling of common struggle among Black Americans. Maybe it was the push for independence by African nations and the residual inspiration that made its way across the Atlantic. Maybe it was that we Negroes had created rock and roll, yet another art form that White America was embracing and co-opting—jacking and then excluding us from—as it continued to keep a safe distance from us while profiting from our genius. Eventually a White dude baptized Elvis Presley would become the "king" of this new thing, in spite of this new thing's nappy Black roots.

By the 1960s this resistance to business as usual had shifted from the move for political change within the system to the move for renewed cultural identity rooted in revolutionary Blackness. Afeni Shakur saw the emergence of a remarkably different Black man: loud, confident, rebellious, as scary to White folks as Richard Wright's Bigger Thomas but smarter, more focused. Staggalee with a ten-point plan. To name the models for this new Black man would require a roll call of Malcolm X, Medgar Evers, Martin Luther King Jr., Robert Williams, James Forman, Stokely Carmichael, H. Rap Brown, Huey Newton, Fred Hampton, George Jackson, and more bad-ass Negroes than I can acknowledge in this here sentence. Afeni confessed to me that one of the main reasons she joined the Black Panther Party was because that was where an army of brothers were, bringing the noise, quoting Marx and Malcolm and Mao Tse-Tung, while rocking a uniform of black turtlenecks, black berets, black sunglasses, and black leather jackets. These were rebels with a cause (Black power!), righteous ride-'em cowboys lining up against FBI don J. Edgar Hoover's G-men and other agents of the oppressive state. (An aside: Ain't it mad strange how many young Black males once wanted to be in the movement—even if only in their fantasies—while nowadays many young brothers want to be hustlers, rappers, ballplayers, pimps, and players? My, how the paradigm has shifted, how the icons of Black manhood have changed. I'ma get back to this point later, trust me.) Where the brothers were, the sisters were, too. Tupac was born from this lovely confluence.

Afeni Shakur had been a Panther, an activist, a revolutionary, and had been arrested with twenty other members (the notorious Panther 21 case) and accused of plotting to blow up important New York City landmarks. Afeni was a native daughter of the "Dirty South," slung into the world via North Carolina as Alice Faye Williams. She told me that, "like everyone else in the early '60s," she initially "watched the Civil Rights Movement on television." She would eventually move north, to New York City, and be confronted with the movement's face and soul through two events: the historic Ocean Hill–Brownsville, Brooklyn, parent-student strike, in which one of her family members was participating, and the formation of a chapter of the Black Panther Party in the Big Apple shortly after it had been founded in Oakland, California, by Huey Newton and Bobby Seale. The movement Afeni had observed on television had morphed from nonviolent protests with colored folks getting fire-hosed to a radical new set of strategies, a new movement that was unapologetically Black in method and language and no longer terrified of the White tribe, of the law, of the system. For a lot of people of Afeni's generation, the new Negro running this new movement blew their minds, made them think a complete overhaul of the whole scheme might just be imminent, finally. This is what I hear from time to time from the old-school Black folks: *Man, we just knew things was about to hit the fan, that America was really going to change into something newer and freer, for everyone.*

What the elders tell me they did not fully grasp or anticipate was how the United States government, via its counterintelligence program, was completely and maniacally determined to shut down the entire freedom ride. It remains unclear to this day which leaders were purposely killed by whom and why, which were set up, set down, or pitted against each other, why some were imprisoned or chased out of the country, why some lost their minds or fell into drink and drugs, and why some simply sold out and bought totally into the system they had so vehemently opposed. But if you wanna get part of the lowdown, I highly recommend you check some of them FBI files. It ain't pretty, pot-na, believe that.

America had never seen Black men such as these, and this new Black man left America as shaken as it had been back when cotton was king and Nat Turner and all them other uppity slave revolters raised Cain back in the 1800s. *Look Out Whitey! Black Power's Gon' Get Your Mama!* asserted the title of one of then radical-chic author Julius Lester's books. Little did they realize that Whitey was heeding the call, looking out.

THIS IS THE universe into which the first part of the hip-hop generation was birthed. Those of us manifested around, say, 1964, 1965, and through about 1980 make up the bulk of this subgroup, the hip-hop generation part one, 'cuz Lawd knows the shorties coming up now ain't known nothin' 'cept a hip-hop America. Anyway, I have often wondered, as I studied Malcolm and Martin, Fannie Lou Hamer, Ella Baker, George Jackson, Angela Davis, Muhammad Ali, Curtis Mayfield, Nina Simone, the Student Nonviolent Coordinating Committee, the Southern Christian Leadership Conference, the Nation of Islam, the Panthers, the US Organization, the sit-ins, the marches, the riots, the Black Arts Movement, all of it, how a baby rolling around his momma's stomach during those mutinous times might have been affected by all that activity and upheaval and chaos. How could that still unformed child *not* have been affected by this stuff? Perhaps this is why my mother tried to abort me not once but twice, her youthful Southern persona downright afraid of bringing a "bastard child" into a society she herself did not remotely comprehend. She too had moved north in the 1960s, as Afeni had—from the backwoods of the Low Country of South Carolina—to secure a better life, and now she was pregnant, and soon thereafter my father would be a ghost, his responsibilities to us as real as his responsibilities to himself: nonexistent. But I survived those abortion attempts—miraculously, given my mother's determination, my aunt Birdie told me a few years ago—and I was born on April 24, 1966, as I have said elsewhere, one year after Malcolm was gunned down, two years before Dr. King was blown away, and five years before Tupac would crawl, face and soul first, onto the earth.

With no daddy in sight, there was no formula, no blueprint for manhood. Nothing. What my mother had to go on was her father, my granddaddy Pearlie, the first man to penetrate her fragile life, who, I would be told as an adult, once slugged my grandmother Lottie so hard that she hit the floor with a thud and lay there unconscious for several minutes. My granddaddy kicked my grandmother, shook her callously, and then finally threw a bucket of water across her face "to loose her from her sleep." Suffice it to say that my granddaddy was a mean and violent man.

America had taught him its meanness and violence very well; he internalized it and took it out on everyone within reach of his coarse tongue and his chubby dark-chocolate fists. My mother, a victim of her father's violence, would in due course victimize me in a similar manner. Every single one of us is a victim, really, the insanity passed down and around like a family heirloom. And if a blueprint for manhood is never given to us or steadfastly fashioned by us, since freedom ain't gonna come from the boss man, how will we ever end this very vicious cycle?

To me that was precisely what the Civil Rights and Black Power movements were about on a personal level: ending the revolving doors of madness. But as Black men of that period affirmed themselves in new and powerful ways, what remained, etched deep into our psyches, was what my homegirl Robyn Rodgers (a.k.a. DJ Reborn) calls "a bootleg definition of White manhood," something we obtained from the White male powerbrokers who've run America since America has been America. Is it any wonder that some of the most dynamic men of the Civil Rights/Black Power epoch were adulterers, liars, thieves, physical and emotional abusers of women, drug or alcohol or sex addicts—in other words, the very embodiment of the spirit they claimed they wanted to seek out and destroy? An uncomfortable question: If these men had been successful at ending racism unequivocally, does it follow logically that they too would have ceased terrorizing each other and Black women? Look at it like this: Yes, Malcolm X and the Honorable Elijah Muhammad, de facto leader of the Nation of Islam (NOI), had a very nasty and very public split. And yes, Malcolm was considered traitorous by many, including some within the NOI rank-and-file and NOI sympathizers, because he aggressively challenged what he felt were Muhammad's ethical shortcomings. Nevertheless, it remains clear, based on the testimony of Malcolm's contemporaries, the evidence amassed by scholars who've made him their subject, and what Malcolm himself says during the last lap of his autobiography, that whoever wanted to kill him was, without a doubt, far greater a force than the Nation of Islam. But even if it was an outside force that pulled the strings, it was a Black man who pulled the trigger. And what kind of man, what kind of *Black* man, is such a self-hating Negro, so drunk with stupidity and a depraved sense of duty, that some external force could make him wrap his niggerized hand (how could he not believe that both he and Malcolm were nothing more than worthless niggas?) around the barrel of a gun and blast away another man, another Black man, a man like Malcolm? In other words, even in the midst of a life-and-death liberation movement, why is it that Black men continued to kill each other, their women, themselves?

This is the scenario that greeted both Tupac Shakur and me at birth, that said, *Come on down, welcome to the terrordome.* I did not really know my father, and Afeni at first was not sure if Tupac's father was Legs, a straight-up gangsta affiliated with legendary drug kingpin Nicky Barnes, or Billy Garland, a member of the Black Panther Party. Afeni, for reasons only she knows, opted to tell

Tupac that Legs was his father. Tupac would find out many years later, long after he had cried as an adolescent over Legs' death, that Billy Garland was in fact his natural father and very much alive. My mother tried desperately, the first eight years of my life, to get my father to contribute something for the boy he had helped to make. He did, at irregular intervals, and then he faded away forever. Legs was around for a while, and then Afeni got with Mutulu Shakur, who was 'Pac's stepfather and father of 'Pac's sister, Sekyiwa. Mutulu would be around until the early 1980s, when he was arrested and later sentenced to sixty years in jail for his involvement in an armored-car robbery. Tupac had two fathers, one a radical political activist who wound up in prison, the other a street hustler who died of a crack-induced heart attack, and these two characters together formed the spiritual nucleus of Tupac's personality. Both here, then gone, just as my pops was here, there, gone. All offering a model of manhood based on absences, inconsistencies, allegiance to the movement, allegiance to the streets, allegiance to selfish and myopic priorities that were more important to them than the boys left behind to sift through the ruins of their battered and bruised lives.

PART II

"Tupac is dead." The words punched hard and below the belt as I sat in a Las Vegas hotel room on the afternoon of Friday, September 13, 1996, watching HBO's umpteenth rerun of Spike Lee's *Malcolm X*. I gazed at my friend Allison Samuels, a *Newsweek* journalist, in astonishment because, unlike the other times I had heard those words during the course of the week, *this* "Tupac is dead" rang with a thunderous finality.

When I'd first heard the news that Tupac Shakur had been shot, I'd thought that it must be a hoax. I said to myself, *He could not have been shot . . . again.* And if indeed 'Pac had been shot for the second time in his public life—the first occurred in New York City in November 1994—surely he would survive, as he had the earlier shelling. While there is still, to this day, debate on how many bullets Tupac actually caught in that first episode (was it five? was it three? had he really been shot in his balls?), what was not contested during Tupac's life was his implausible resiliency, his tenacity, his larger-than-life antihero heroism. America has always deified mortals who could suffer through any crisis, triumph over it, and even, to the shame of the rest of us very human weaklings, toss sand in the face of death itself. There is no denying that many of us who heard that Tupac had been capped a second time believed, genuinely, that it was not a big deal, that he would once more recover to talk *ish* another day. But Tupac, this go-round, had been struck badly, and the barrage of bullets, on the evening of Saturday, September 7, in Las Vegas, was far more severe than the New York City gunfire. Although Tupac would wage war against death, like the soldier he was, for several days, leading many of us to conclude he would cross safely back over to life, he expired from injuries caused by the gunshot wounds to his chest. The official cause of his death, at twenty-five, was respiratory failure and cardio-pulmonary arrest.

After that first stuttering conversation in Atlanta, I had the opportunity to interview Tupac in person several times more, in various parts of the country and in various settings—at the infamous Rikers Island jail complex in New York City, at a barbeque joint in Los Angeles' South Central, at his home outside Atlanta, Georgia—and I had come to know him rather well. I had become, for better or worse, the media's "expert" on Tupac Shakur, whatever that means. What I do know is that with the news of his death, I was as psychologically wounded as I had ever been in my life. I could not believe that hip-hop's greatest icon was dead, gone, reduced to an armful of assorted memories. For some reason I could not cry—not there, not right then. I do not know what I felt beyond an immediate and intense hurt. *Has hip-hop come to this?* Rock and roll has had its martyrs—Buddy Holly, Janis Joplin, and John Lennon, among dozens of others—whose deaths were all the more difficult because they seemed like random, star-crossed accidents. Now hip-hop was beginning to have its own martyrs, whose deaths were anything but random—Eazy-E, dead from AIDS, Tupac Shakur, dead from gunshot blasts . . .

BUT REALLY, HIP-HOP was born into death, mayhem, and violence. Once again, we cannot separate the civil rights and hip-hop generations, although many of us from one side of the tracks or the other have attempted, mightily, to do so—including me, idiotically. Hip-hop was the movement that rose from the ashes of the Civil Rights/Black Power movement's flameout.

Hip-hop was manifested in the ghettos of America, in New York City more than anywhere else, in the late 1960s and the early 1970s. It has always been a male-centered art form, largely because the Civil Rights Movement, at least on the surface, was so male-centered: Malcolm X, Martin Luther King Jr., Bayard Rustin, Roy Wilkins, Whitney Young, Stokely Carmichael, H. Rap Brown, LeRoi Jones (later Amiri Baraka), Huey Newton, Cassius Clay (later Muhammad Ali), James Baldwin, and dozens of other local, regional, and national "stars" of that period. Yes, Black women were there as well, plotting strategies, doing the grunt work, marching and singing songs, making signs, clenching their teeth and their fists, getting bombed and dragged and fire-hosed and clocked with rocks across the skull right alongside the brothers. The women, without question, were leaders in their own right. But it was the brothers, in my humble opinion, who represented the direct and immediate threat to the White male power structure. Since the United States has always been a patriarchal nation, when Black people finally mustered the collective nerve to resist the domestic terrorism, from the mid-1950s through the start of the 1970s, it was Black men who posed the most serious threat to White men. European men, after centuries of colonialism and exploitation, had come to defend their actions and define their manhood by what they could rule and regulate and, if necessary, annihilate. The Civil Rights Movement raised the skirt on the good old White men's network. The basis of their reality—White supremacy—was being called into question, and White men were being asked to share power for the first time, forced to own up to the country's founding creed.

White men had up to that point been unquestioned. Unquestioned in their right to write history, to wage "just" wars, to invent the magical devices that pushed civilization forward (or take credit for the inventions of others), to discover and triumph over rough terrain, to induce "primitives" to accept civilization and a god who just happened to look like that same White man's kinfolk. This, they declared, was their duty, their burden, their manifest destiny, and their birthright. But now, with the rise of the Black Power movement, the moment they'd seen in their nightmares seemed to have finally arrived, the moment when some of those misguided, and unappreciative natives got restless and decided to take a piece of the throne they helped build. Their resistance was a challenge to a model of manhood, their way of saying that this unquestioned power over their lives was no longer acceptable, that the throne needed to be flipped over, even if the White man was still sitting on the damned thing.

While this rebellious spirit of colored folks was feared in general, it was the Black men who principally got the White man's goat, because they were perceived as having an interest beyond freedom from the White man's structure. They were perceived as wanting to *replace* that structure. Visions of slave rebellions, of Black men taking the sex of White women, of Black behinds sitting in the master's chair, made their way into a certain White imagination, and one thing became clear, right then and there, to these powerful men sick with their own power: These Black men had to be stopped, arrested, chased out of the country, driven crazy, fired, harassed, shot at, killed while they were awake (Martin Luther King Jr.) or while they were asleep (Fred Hampton and Mark Clark). It did not matter whether it was done by some poor, working-class White man (James Earl Ray), racist White police officers, or a Black man loyal to the system. What does matter, dear reader, is that those orders and those actions did happen. Those murders happened. And the rebellion was broken. I *wish* none of this were true, that none of this were a part of the American saga, but alas, it is.

THE CIVIL RIGHTS Movement did lead to some important political and emotional and spiritual victories. What would this country look like today if the movement had *not* happened? Would the Whites in power have come to their senses and said, "Gosh, ya know, it is just not right that we tell the Negroes to sit at the back of the bus, to drink from this rusty water faucet, to enter through that back door, to accept second-class citizenship and an inferiority complex"? That is asking a lot of people who had been conditioned by their socialization process—their school, their church, their family, and their God—to suddenly shift their thinking, to turn inside out on their own. For that reason I do feel blessed, truly, that I am not in the position of my grandfather, who was illiterate chiefly because of the stunted reality of his upbringing in the Jim Crow South and who, I am told, was so terrified of White people that he did not vote, even though he was able to do so, because in the secluded, shimmering darkness of his mind he felt that even marking an X on voting papers would upset the good White people of his dingy South Carolina town. Truth is, he was probably right.

I feel blessed because I have been able to trudge through a school system and obtain something resembling an education. My mother reminds me, often and loudly, that I have gone farther in school than she (a very mediocre grade-school education) and my maternal grandparents (no formal schooling whatsoever), and I even had, thanks to a program created during the civil rights battles, the opportunity to attend college (the program is called the Educational Opportunity Fund in my native New Jersey). And I do not both fear and despise White people the way a lot of my elders do. I am very much like a lot of heads in the hip-hop generation: I am not going to smile, shuffle, or give a good goddamn what anyone thinks about me, and that most assuredly includes White folks.

Which is not to say I hate White folks. Hate and fear are interconnected; you cannot have one without the other. Indeed, fear is what fuels and propels hate. Fear in turn stems from ignorance. It has been a difficult excursion for me to get to a point of being able to say this, given how profoundly miseducated I had been, and given my initial reactions to White people once I began to see their collective history from top to bottom, minus the mythologies and convenient revisions. The most revolutionary thing any of us can do is search for truth, real, raw truth, and learn to love ourselves and to discover the possibilities of common, universal humanity lurking at our fingertips. And not in some lame, politically correct, we-are-the-world way, but in a way that embraces our commonality while still demanding accountability for what history has wrought, what the present is raining down upon us, and what tomorrow can be, for better or worse.

And what I love, in spite of the typical struggle of my impoverished childhood and the deep self-hatred I carted around into my adult years, is the ability to say I love my Black self, in spite of being taught, from the moment I was able to conceive a thought, to hate my Black self. What an internal revolution that has been, and still is! But a major part of that process of shedding self-hatred comes from freeing my own voice to speak the truth of what I see around me, inside of me. What I *do* hate, despise, detest, is oppression in any shape or form, any force that seeks to stifle the voice that liberated me—my own. Once more, I say what I feel, when I feel it, and exactly how I feel it. This, too, is how Tupac Shakur rolled. As did Ice Cube, Chuck D., and other voices of hip-hop before 'Pac. And others after Tupac. I have no doubt that the outspokenness—be it political or apolitical—that is so discernible in hip-hop today is the residual effect of the bluntness of the latter part of the Civil Rights Movement.

The Civil Rights Movement cannot be underestimated. It was as powerful a force for change as has ever occurred in American history or even the history of the modern world. Its gains were numerous and concrete. It must also be said, however, that in spite of civil rights and voting rights bills, in spite of the alleged explosion of the Black middle class, in spite of more Black folks on television and in films during the first half of the 1970s, in spite of Blacks being allowed (without the presence of the National Guard) into historically White colleges, universities, and public schools, in spite of the rise in the number of Black elected officials, Blacks in corporate America, and Blacks in newsrooms (someone with some melanin had to cover them riots), in spite of the birth of a funkier kind of Black music with a message, and in spite of the gigantic Afros, the dashikis, *Soul Train,* and so on—in spite of all this, what Dr. King worried about toward the end of his life was, categorically, taking place. That is, not only were the Black poor being left behind, but the door was being slammed on them—for good, it appeared. Which is why Dr. King was in Memphis when he was killed in April 1968, attempting to rally support for sanitation workers, working-class folks; to me it was a way of saying, *I may be privileged, but what good does isolated privilege mean if my people continue to suffer as a whole?* And which is why Dr. King, notwithstanding his heavily credentialed middle-class background, was attempting to organize a Poor People's Campaign. He understood, better than most leaders then or now, that the ability to sit anywhere on a bus or at a lunch counter next to White people portends nothing if one does not have the money for a bus ride or a meal, or if the goal down the long road to real freedom is not to own the bus company or the restaurant. But King was killed, and to me—regardless of what Jesse Jackson has said and done, regardless of what Ralph Abernathy (King's right-hand man during his years on the front lines) tried to do, regardless of the soaring, operatic rhetoric of Louis Farrakhan and the public pronouncements of the NAACP or the annual state-of-Black-America reports of the National Urban League, regardless of Al Sharpton's marches and protests and presidential aspirations—no *national* Black leader and no *national* Black organization since the 1960s has made a serious and sustained effort to help the poor in our communities or in America as a whole. *None.*

This is why I declare, nonstop, and mad loud so you old Negro leaders, deficient in the art of listening, can hear me: Tupac Shakur *dead* is more relevant to poor and struggling young Black people in America than a Jesse Jackson or an Al Sharpton *alive.* The perception is the reality: There ain't no national agenda for Black folks and ain't nobody really been trying to create one for the past thirty years and Black America ain't as dumb as you all think we are as you all dart from one TV camera and one photo opportunity to the next. This much we know: From the beauty of the freedom movement, then, we have a big Black nothing, today.

It was this vacuum that partially called into itself the birth of the hip-hop nation. For hip-hop is a reaction to institutionalized White racism, American classism, the material, spiritual, and psychological failures of the Civil Rights Movement, the United States government's abandonment of its war on poverty, the horrendous lack of vision and incompetence of "traditional" Black leadership, the Black middle class moving away and forgetting its poor relatives in the 'hood (a small percentage of us got out and moved on up like the TV-land Jeffersons, but what about the rest of us?), the fiscal crises of urban centers like New York City in the 1970s, and the grossly stark belief that if the poor African Americans, West Indians, and Puerto Ricans who spawned hip-hop did not create something to preoccupy themselves, to give them an option other than death, to give them a voice, some visibility, a space to breathe, they would surely die.

Those raucous, angry, cocksure Black males had upset White America so much in the 1960s that it seemed as if Black women were permitted to venture into arenas to explore economically, with jobs and other opportunities, where Black men were not allowed. And the chorus sang again: Black men and Black women are oppressed equally but differently, ya dig? And most working-class Black men who were left behind—the Kool Hercs, the Afrika Bambaataas, the Grandmaster Flashes, the Pete DJ Jones, all the founding fathers and pioneers of hip-hop, men who are at the moment in their forties and even fifties—formed hip-hop culture mainly because their spirits and the chants of the ancestors told them they had to make something out of nothing. That, to me, is why hip-hop has been so male-centered, so attributable to the Black male persona (even with the monumental contributions of our Latino brethren), really from its inception.

Hip-hop was an act of recognition, on some level, that while the Civil Rights Movement had altered America and opened up some doors for a smidgen of the community, the vast majority of us were cemented in the ghettos of America. And these ghettos were worse than ever. At least prior to the civil rights era, middle-class Blacks and poor Blacks lived in the same 'hood, and thus a kid on the block could still see possibilities of a better life, if not in his house, then next door, across the street, up the block. For example, if you did not have a daddy around, someone else's daddy was your daddy. If you did not have a doctor in your household, or a lawyer, or a teacher, there was sure to be one up the street. These things were visible, tangible, and so none of them seemed impossible, remote, unreal. Hip-hop was formed as our communities were splintering, fragmenting, disintegrating, thanks in part to the rush toward integration. Not only did some of us colored folks integrate physically, we integrated our souls and our minds, leaving behind our less fortunate brothers and sisters to fend for themselves. This brings to mind that scene from the film *Titanic* where the advantaged folks scramble to save themselves while the grimy, deprived people remained locked behind a fence at the bottom of the boat and would have to either drown or swim. Folks trapped in the concrete boxes we call ghettos on the heels of the Civil Rights Movement could have completely drowned, and many have. Yet hip-hop, a truly organic art form and culture created by poor people, by people from the bottom, like jazz or the blues before it, spoke to this isolation, this alienation, this sense that many of us had been forgotten, cast off, thrown in the trash bin of so-called civilization.

So we took what we had, our parents' record collection, a turntable, no, two turntables, a microphone, spray paint, markers, cardboard from the nearby deli, pieces of linoleum from our mothers' kitchens, and we boys, we men, gave the world us, hip-hop, the new Black thing. It happened as I was entering kindergarten, as Tupac Shakur was being born, as Marvin Gaye was asking the question "What's Going On," as the Temptations were singing "Papa Was a Rolling Stone," as some of us were dying in Vietnam or returning from Vietnam to die another sort of death back home, a slow procession of death through our bodies, across our faces, on the fingers that held liquor bottles, in the veins that trembled as a needle angled downward and into the bloodstream, as we were being changed from wanna-be Black Panthers into wanna-be hustlers like the Mack and Superfly, and as it became clear that White folks and Black folks, crackers and niggas equally, were scared of revolution.

Simply put, it is the American way to be unequivocally in line with the program, even if the program is squashing or denying aspects of your humanity. Be out of line, be a bad nigga, and watch the wrath of that system come down upon your head, homie.

Yes this was the world that hip-hop was born into—that I was born into. As a result, when I encounter older Black men in this day and age, men old enough to be my father, men who lived through a segregated America and the bloody and brutal social orgy that was the 1960s, I wonder to myself what they survived and what they perpetually tote with them. Was he a baby-faced soldier in Vietnam meticulously blowing away countless Vietcong because he had been told to do so and because if he didn't he might have returned to America in a body bag? Was he an overall-wearing civil rights worker in Mississippi, Alabama, or somewhere else in the Deep South, who had withstood the insults, the pokes and prods, the death threats? Is he still carrying scars from all of that, akin to a person who has survived a series of bombings, except in this brother's case the bombings were inward, psychological and spiritual? Is he a working-class hero, someone who has worked with his hands or his back or both his entire life, his smile and his body ever ready by day, his anger taken out at night on his woman or his children or his buddies or some stray person beside him at the local bar, on the bus, on the subway, at his place of work? Is he, in effect, committing slow suicide because his life was reduced to a sentence of hard labor, surviving from paycheck to paycheck, from one humiliation to the next, the color of his skin as cumbersome as the weight of trying to be the man of the house when he still has to pay rent to someone else? Is he one of the members of the Black middle class who endured the lunacy of those times and did well for himself by the standards of the so-called American dream, with the house, the car or two, the good job, the latest gadgets, yet has lurking somewhere on his soul a cancerous blemish where he compromised portions of himself—his sanity, his dignity, his identity— to get ahead materially, a sacrifice his ancestors could not have foreseen? Was he real with himself? Does he understand why Black men of my generation, perhaps even his own son or sons, feel he is a sellout, that he is a coward, that he acts like a White man, talks like a White man, thinks like a White man because, fundamentally, he has surrendered his own soul? And what of that older Black man who has remained on the front lines of what we term "the struggle," the one who has an African or Muslim name, the one who wears Afrocentric clothing, who has maybe dreaded his hair, who to this day insists on labeling Black people as "sister" and "brother," who is routinely called "Baba" by his fellow Afrocentrists, who instinctually refers to White people, underneath his breath and when among his like-minded peers, as "crackers" or "devils," who mocks the police as "pigs," and who is so out of touch with the hip-hop generation, including his own children, that he thinks these children and their culture an aberration, their culture, their music, completely without soul, artless, chaotic, noisy, foul, despicable, ruthless, ugly? Why does he not take into account, given how astute he is, how completely without soul, artless, chaotic, noisy, foul, despicable, ruthless, and ugly the conditions were that created and help to perpetuate the music and culture of his children? Or does he even care? Does he not want to look in the mirror of his children's eyes because he might see himself, so terribly self-righteous, so terribly flawed, and so terribly naked?

And what of any of these types of Black men, of that civil rights and Black-power era, who are in such a state of arrested development that they cannot even begin to comprehend and appreciate and learn from the herstories told by their female peers with names like bell hooks, Angela Davis, Kathleen Cleaver, Alice Walker, Toni Morrison, Ntozake Shange, Sonia Sanchez, Toni Cade Bambara, Audre Lorde, and many, many other sisters? Black men who feel any talk of the rights of Black women is an attack on Black men, on their manhood, or, some state defiantly, a clear-cut collusion with the White man, even as these Black men ignore the fact that some of them have raped Black women, lied to Black women, manipulated Black women, beaten Black women, killed, in some form or another, Black women, all under the guise of maintaining some twisted notion of their power, rank, and authority in our communities. This was the spectrum of flawed manhood that the hip-hop generation was met with at its inception.

But the flaws in that generation of Black men all come back to how manhood in America is established: More often than not, it is based on conquest, subjugating, dominating, and abandoning others, while paying no further price. Men are applauded for their machismo, their grit, their toughness. Show any level of sensitivity, shed a tear or two in public, display any feelings that have nothing to do with winning, and you are reduced to being a "sucker," a "punk," a "pussy," or a "fag," your sexuality thoroughly interrogated while your ego is being riddled with hollow-point innuendos. Those men with the power get to tell powerless men what manhood is, modeled after themselves or whatever tall tales they have spun about themselves.

It goes without saying that White men, particularly *wealthy* White men, have had a grip on this prime-time slot for a very long time and ain't trying to give it up, no matter how in vogue Black culture is in this preliminary phase of the twenty-first century, or was during the 1920s or the 1960s and early 1970s. At the end of the day it remains a constant, regrettably, that there is some White man somewhere in the stratosphere who, methodically, calls the shots and still signs the checks no matter how much we cheer the "success" and "power" and "juice" of Colin Powell, Tiger Woods, Michael Jordan, Kenneth Chenault, Magic Johnson, Russell Simmons, Damon Dash, Bill Cosby, Sean "P. Diddy" Combs, Jesse Jackson, Earl Graves, or Richard Parsons. The rule remains marginalization, which creates its own pathologies.

That is why I have some degree of respect for Russell Simmons, founder of Def Jam Records and hip-hop's first music mogul, more than ever these days. He has enough sense to realize he is still outside the building, notwithstanding all that he has done for over twenty years and counting—a record label, a clothing line, TV and film projects, philanthropic work, a political action committee, a Broadway show—to help to make hip-hop culture *the* American culture of our times. Russell has stated publicly and privately that all his millions have not gotten him ownership of the metaphorical building, or even a place inside it. And that is precisely why it was so tragically disturbing to read a *Rolling Stone* article about a year or so ago in which Damon Dash, head of Roc-a-fella Records (Jay-Z is his partner and biggest star), and Irv Gotti, overseer of Murder, Inc., were arguing over which of the two was "the hottest nigga in the building." The building belongs to the Universal Music Group, which owns the Island Def Jam Music Group, both of which own chunks of Roc-a-fella and Murder, Inc. "The hottest nigga in the building"? That is like deliberating over which slave is preferred by the slave master. And this battle royal was between Dash, a product of prep schools, and Gotti, who until just a few years ago was considered a sort of nerdish dude who DJed and produced a few decent underground records. In other words, this was an argument between two Black men who have been exposed to enough of the world beyond the narrow trappings of ghettocentricity to know better but who have consciously decided that in order to be perceived as men, as *the* man, they have to don the worst attributes of ghetto life and American manhood, even at the price of resembling a pair of foul-mouthed minstrels in the pages of *Rolling Stone*.

But strange things are happening everywhere in these

last days. The broken links between two generations of Black men have led to some odd phenomena. When I look at the name Roc-a-fella and the names Irv Gotti and Murder, Inc., I have to scratch my walnut head and wonder why Black males in hip-hop today, in America today, name themselves and/or their urban boutique companies after powerful White men or White mobsters of yesteryear, rather than after great Black entrepreneurs like, say, the late Reginald Lewis or, as a minimum requirement, after a Black gangsta figure from somewhere in *our* history, like Nicky Barnes. But it inevitably goes back to power, or rather having the power to dictate who should be remembered and how they will be represented in popular culture, in history, in our collective consciousness, and who will be marginalized. In the absence of a steely bond between generations of Black men, definitions of power devolve to outside forces, like the media giants who control global cultural output. If they want crime figures to be an integral part of how American manhood is composed, then it will be so, even if it is a fictitious, made-up character like Al Pacino's Tony "Scarface" Montana or HBO's Tony Soprano. What matters is that the character exudes the basic qualities of the American man: competitive fire, ruthless machismo, patriarchy run amok, extreme misogyny, zero tolerance for disrespect (perceived or real), a love of money, and violence (by whatever means necessary) as the primary technique by which to obtain power. And that's a power within our grasp that we've surrendered. Power means you are the shaper, you are the builder, you are the dictionary, you are the one who defines everything within your jurisdiction. Power means you own something out-right, which is why I have more respect for Oprah Winfrey, a Black woman, than I do for the legions of "successful" Black men who run around flossing their wares, pretend-ing to be empowered but owning nothing except maybe their homes, their cars, their two-ways, their power suits, and percentages of whatever company they started or run for someone else. Meanwhile Oprah owns her television show, owns the studio in which her television show is pro-duced, and owns more things than most Black people would ever know or would want to know, because far too many of us have made peace with being ignorant. So what kind of power have you got, as a man, if the very way you define yourself comes from outside your environment, your domain, your soul? Once more, people often confuse power and influence. And history tells us that the system will tol-erate Black men who work for and within its walls, who do not question or buck the system, who instead are cheer-leaders for the status quo, and who do not say, like Martin Luther King Jr. or Malcolm X, that the system needs to be turned on its stringy head and the filth shaken from its pockets. When the tradition of struggle and remembrance breaks, the past is forgotten and the system triumphs.

As ALLISON, MY journalist friend, gathered her tape re-corder and notepad and fought back her tears, I let out a hefty sigh as I sat there staring at the television set, watching Denzel Washington play Malcolm X, who felt he had been played by the Honorable Elijah Muhammad. Of course, the irony of inhaling a film about one icon and his life and death as I was being told that another icon had died was not lost on me. I will say it again: Perhaps rather naively, I had not expected Tupac to die. Not like this, gunned down while riding in a car with Death Row Records CEO Marion "Suge" Knight a few hours after a Mike Tyson bout in Las Vegas. Tupac was sitting in the passenger seat as Knight steered the black tinted-window BMW while an entourage of ten other cars followed. A white Cadillac eased up beside the black BMW and a volley of thirteen gunshots ripped through the night air, four of them chomping Tupac's chocolate-covered flesh. Knight allegedly escaped with a very minor bruise to his head, but Tupac was seriously injured. He had his right lung removed and was placed in a medically induced coma to rest his traumatized body. Tupac held on for one day, then two, then three, and there were whispers that his condition was improving. I remember phoning 'Pac's girlfriend at the time, Kidada Jones (daughter of Quincy Jones), who was either in Vegas or on her way to Vegas, and she'd assured me that he was going to make it. Her confidence had made me believe. But Tupac Shakur was dead. As dead as Denzel's Malcolm X would be when he entered the Audubon Ballroom on that day. I snapped the television off and headed to the hospital.

The word had traveled quickly, via cellular phone, fax, beeper, and e-mail. By the time I got to the University

Medical Center of Southern Nevada, a throng of well-wishers turned mourners, mostly young and Black and very much around the way, stood inside and outside the trauma center where Tupac had been hospitalized for the past six days. Some wept hysterically, some stared into space, and others sipped on everything from bottled water to malt liquor. A few homies spilled their brew on the ground in honor of Tupac. All makes of SUVs and cars rode ominously across the intersection of Goldring Avenue and Rose Street, converting the blocks encompassing the hospital into Las Vegas' version of Los Angeles' Crenshaw Boulevard on a Sunday night. Tupac's music blasted from some of the vehicles, while others, particularly one black Hummer, rolled by silently, the young men inside slouched in their seats, gazing vacantly in the direction of the hospital. Even though it was September, the Las Vegas temperature easily soared above 100 degrees, and there was a thick, portentous feeling in the air. Reports that there had already been retaliation for Tupac's murder stutter-stepped through the crowd. For that and other reasons, Las Vegas police, in black-and-white patrol cars and the on-foot gang unit, smothered the area. And the media—television crews, newspaper stringers, magazine reporters, radio dispatchers, freelance photographers—worked the outer perimeter of the horde, absorbing the sights and sounds of anyone who would comment or pose flashing the "W" hand signal of the West Coast on behalf of Tupac. The scene felt eerie, like a makeshift funeral procession. When a black Lexus drove up to the hospital's entrance, the throng and the media personnel jointly paused to see who it was. The mammoth figure of Suge Knight materialized from the passenger side smoking a cigar. Knight walked slowly into the hospital with three other men, his face emotionless. Nevertheless, the young Black men in the waiting area flocked to Knight, including Death Row's teenage singer Danny Boy, the only one in the contingent to weep openly. The crew did a group hug for a moment, then quickly pulled apart. When Knight was told that Tupac's body had already been removed from the hospital, he and his boys made their way unhurriedly back to the Lexus. Knight didn't appear to be too concerned with his own safety, in spite of rumors that he too was a target of whoever had shot Tupac. As some media folk stood behind the hospital window right behind Knight when he climbed into the Lexus, they joked that they too would be shot if someone suddenly let loose on Knight. A sigh went up when Knight and his buddies drove off.

The shock waves swept the country for the rest of the night, throughout the weekend, and into the subsequent weeks—and picked up more steam when the Notorious B.I.G., 'Pac's alleged rival, was gunned down in Los Angeles in March 1997. "Who killed Tupac?" and all the meanings that could possibly be attached to that question had become the topic of banter on radio programs, on television talk shows, on college campuses, at Tupac memorials, in special magazine tributes, on the Internet, in one television special or straight-to-video documentary after another, and at record stores where Tupac's albums—old

CDs and posthumous "new" CDs—sold to people who a few weeks earlier hadn't even known who Tupac was—or who didn't believe he was, for-real for-real, dead.

Tupac Shakur is a symbol of my generation's angst and rage, and in death he is more famous than he was alive. Dead, he has sold far more records than he did while alive, which says much about the worth of the breathing life of a Black man in America. Because of the controversies and misunderstandings that often surrounded his every move, Tupac Shakur—like James Dean and Donny Hathaway, or Jimi Hendrix and Jim Morrison, or, yes, like Malcolm X—remains an enigma to many, many people. I cannot say that I really knew Tupac, although some people might think I did because of the many conversations I had with him. What I do know is that Tupac's numerous public personalities were emblematic of Black men, both working-poor Black men and middle-class Black men, younger Black men and older Black men, and it is ludicrous to hear Black men of whatever ilk cruelly and crudely attack Tupac as if there are not elements of his plethora of personas riding through each of our psyches. If Tupac was angry and not able to tell the difference between proactive anger and reactive anger, I say, cousin, that is a gang of us. If Tupac displayed violent, me-against-the-world tendencies, he was only displaying a spirit I've seen in so many Black men in my travels across America—a spirit I have been forced to acknowledge within myself during the frequent full stops on my own life journey. If Tupac was one moment scholarly, then completely ignorant the next, well, hell, that is many of us as well—autodidacts and college grads alike, still looking for truth.

The point I am getting at is that most of us are as lost and contradictory as Tupac himself, forced to discover manhood through trial and error and odd angles—a father or stepfather here, an uncle there, a sports coach over here, some figure from popular culture (music, TV, or film) way over there. I am not trying to dis older Black men in America, but I can count on one hand the elder brothers I have met who:

- are seriously self-critical, the way Malcolm X was, even with his shortcomings
- are vehemently antipatriarcal and antisexist and thus willing to say that we need to think of some new and progressive ways of defining manhood, other than as conquerors and/or pimps, regardless of what form that conquering or pimping takes
- understand that manhood is a lot more than being or proclaiming oneself the man of the house, the bread-winner, the caretaker
- understand that manhood has everything to do with striving to be a whole human being, one who can be both hard and soft, loud and silent, courageous and vulnerable, and not afraid to show or admit these traits
- deem and relate to women as their equals, without hesitation
- are not locked, intellectually, emotionally, or spiritually, into a bygone era or a tired ideology

In other words, if most White men in America are stuck in a state of arrested development, I think it goes without saying that most Black men are as well, and that means all generations, not just the hip-hop generation, son.

So when a Tupac Shakur comes along and says to his father's generation, "I am your child," implicit in that declaration is the notion that you cannot simply reject him as crazy or violent or death-wishing because, in point of fact, he is a mirror reflection of *you*, because he comes from your flesh, your blood, your bone, your sperm, man. What did you teach him, by your actions or inactions, by your presence, by your absence? What kind of manhood you got, where did you get it from, who said it was right, and why? And if, again, Tupac was born in New York City to a mother just out of prison, and was uncertain about who his natural father was, and moved from place to place in his truncated life, and watched his mother, a proud, strong, defiant woman, succumb to a debilitating crack addiction even with her genius and her political activist background, and was a sensitive child, with overtly feminine features and mannerisms, taunted by relatives, peers, neighbors, because he was "too pretty," "too girlish"—why on God's bloody earth would you expect this young Black male, who only made it to age twenty-five (go look and see what Malcolm X, born Malcolm Little, was doing at age twenty-five, then come back and holla at me, aiight?), to be anything other than what he was: a marvelously talented but appallingly schizophrenic and paranoid young man who drank too much, smoked too many cigarettes and too much marijuana, loved women but sometimes acted as if he abhorred them completely, and identified mightily with the poor and underprivileged but had no problem showing off his money, his cars, his clothes, and his jewelry because, fuh shizzle, who wants to be poor without end, particularly in a nation like America where the lifestyles of the rich and famous are rammed down our throats damn near every second via our television sets?

In a sense, then, Tupac Shakur represented—and represents, because God knows his spirit will never die, and because too many of us just won't let the brother go—all that is right and all that is wrong with how we define manhood in America, and specifically what is so wickedly off-kilter about Black manhood in this new millennium, when the behaviors that define manhood are reduced to guns and violence, drugs and alcohol, the objectification and hatred of women, excessive materialism and extreme individualism, hate above love, insensitivity before butt-naked feelings, screwing instead of passionate lovemaking. Tupac Shakur once wrote a song called "Keep Ya Head Up," an emotional anthem dedicated to Black women that bit a line from the chorus of a song his mother may have hummed as a young woman: *Ooh child, things are gonna be easier.* Tupac Shakur also allowed a woman to give him a blowjob in a New York City nightclub, left the club to have sex with her in his hotel room, then left that room when his homies barged in to run a train on that woman, becoming complicit in the worst sort of inhumanity.

No, for the record, I do not think that Tupac Shakur

actually raped that young woman *himself*—never did, never will.

What I do feel happened, as Tupac told me in an infamous Rikers Island interview, is this: He was guilty of not stopping his homies from coming into that hotel room because his backward definition of manhood said if he did that, it would have meant he liked this woman in some way beyond seeing her as a groupie, and that would have meant the scorn of his homeboys. Why would a man with the brilliance and outward swagger of Tupac Shakur suddenly feel compelled to place the love and support of his male friends above that of the safety and sanity of a woman he had been intimate with? Why did he become so weak and cowardly that even as he knew what he was doing was wrong in his heart and in his gut, he ignored that truth, discarded it like garbage, and plowed ahead? He decided, at that moment, that the path to manhood was in doing what the boys do rather than risking their disapproval to stand up for what he felt was right. Not having a blueprint means improvising at every step, sometimes leaping to brilliance, other times to chaos, other times to gross error. This is really not just about Tupac Shakur. This is about all of us.

And it is really about how we men, we Black men, in the context of hip-hop, are so powerless in relation to White America, in relation to White American men (who many of us, dumbly, aspire to emulate), that we, at every turn, oppress women, Black women, by our despicable name-calling ("bitch," "ho," "gold-digger," "chickenhead," etc.), and by our despicable actions (domestic violence, rape, and sexual assault). What we fail to understand is that when we Black men view Black women only as sexual objects, as impediments to our progress, as our enemies, is that we have internalized the very same stereotypes and hatreds the larger White society has had about Black women, dating back to slavery: that Black women are immoral, oversexed, greedy for money and material things, and never to be trusted, while White women, who Black male hip-hoppers *rarely* critique in our music or in our vernacular, are seen as purer, higher, untouchable, which, to some extent, explains the Black male fascination with very light-complexioned Black women, light-skinned Latina women, or Asian women, even, in our music videos. Fully developed and diversified Black womanhood is not acceptable to many of us because it threatens our perceived power. It is much easier to reduce Black women to sexual objects because it allows us to maintain our control, our manhood, if you will. Moreover, the fact that Tupac, although he admitted he was wrong for not stopping his homies from coming into that hotel room, could say to me that the incident convinced him that "there are bitches and there are sisters" says that we Black men in hip-hop have fashioned this ridiculous extreme of what Black women are in our minds: either "queens" or "bitches" with no in-between, no depth, no complexities, no realities other than to service Black men in one way or the other: "queens" work for the king and "bitches" work for the "niggas." What is the difference, friend? Men still rule in both equations. This backward logic explains why Black male leaders rushed to support the eternally troubled Mike Tyson over a decade ago after Desiree Washington charged him with rape (do any of you even care to wonder how Ms. Washington has been doing all these years later after being branded a "traitor" by colored folks?), then, even worse, gave Tyson a rally in Harlem upon his release from prison. Time has proven that Tyson, not Washington, was the one with psychological problems, but, interestingly enough, that chorus of Black male voices is on mute when it comes to encouraging Tyson to seek real help. Or what of the R. Kelly matter, where it has been rumored for years that the R&B crooner has had a thing for female minors, yet we, men *and* women, still support him—as evidenced earlier this year when his latest album, *Chocolate Factory,* bumped the hottest rapper in America, 50 Cent, from the top of the Billboard pop charts. Not only have I heard a number of Black men say that they watched the infamous videotape allegedly showing Kelly engaging in sex with a child, but these Black men saw nothing wrong with it, and some even suggested that "She must have wanted it" or "Well, she looked grown," which says, to me, in the main, that we have become so warped by our powerlessness, our self-hatreds, our hatreds of Black women, that we will rationalize *any* sickening behavior that one from our ranks does because we feel it is our birthright as men to have the sexual favors of women, of girls, even if it means taking it forcibly. And because speaking out against someone from our ranks—a Mike Tyson, a Tupac Shakur, an R. Kelly—portends that we are part of the White establishment attack on Black manhood, that we don't understand (!) that Black men are an endangered species. Well, does being silent around foul Black male behavior mean it is cool to recklessly disregard the sanity and the lives of Black women because we feel they are not as endangered as we are? And what, dear reader, was my mother if she, with her grade-school education, her poverty, her limited skills, and her battles with my father, the community, and the power structure as symbolized by the welfare and housing agencies, raising me alone, with no help, no love, was *not* an endangered species?

Black men in the United States need to come to grips with this hardcore reality: we are virtually powerless, landless, and moneyless, while White manhood has always been measured by these acquisitions, from Andrew Carnegie to Ted Turner. So although we live in a patriarchal society, that is, a male-dominated social order, given the definitions of manhood that loom over us, we are paralyzed, quite literally, from figuring out where we fit in, how we obtain power and privilege, and how we can do so *without* brutalizing and oppressing Black women in the process. But sadly, most of us are not there, so for Black men, that power and privilege is symbolized by our grabbing of the pistol and the penis, and has been, long before hip-hop jumped on the scene with a gangsta lean. If you do not think so, do yourself a favor and check out the old-school blues of Robert Johnson or John Lee Hooker. Or note that Miles Davis had a history of beating Black women and bragged about brutalizing Cicely Tyson in his autobiography. So young Black men of this era have no patent on women-hating behavior. What hip-hop has done, thanks in part to the advent of music videos, is accelerate and exacerbate the violence and the woman-hating to the world stage, a stage that now says, without remorse, that we would rather condemn Black women, which is a sucker move, than challenge the true source of our perpetual misery, the White male power structure, as illustrated by, say, racist police officers, politicians, TV show commentators, multinational corporations, government agencies, and elsewhere. And the White male power structure, sitting on the sidelines watching Black men bash Black women ad infinitum, conveniently washes its hands of blood, guilt, and complicity and spitefully declares that all things hip-hop is what is morally wrong with America—the sexism, the violence, the materialism, and so on—without ever owning up to the fact that sexism, violence, and materialism have existed, and will continue to exist, in the American matrix long after hip-hop fades as an art form.

PART III

Manhood in America is in crisis and has been for quite a long time. The drive behind the things we use to define manhood—excellence at sports, at business, at war—has often curdled into viciousness, rape, and self-destruction when unchecked. Note the number of American military men, regardless of their racial background, who have been recently charged with the beating or killing of their female companions. Check out the Gulf War veterans like Oklahoma City bomber Timothy McVeigh (White), or the man in Arizona (Latino) who killed three of his college professors and then turned the gun on himself. Or peep the fact that one of the men said to be the notorious D.C. snipers of 2002 (Black) was a veteran of the Gulf War as well. We like to think Vietnam was the only war that drove some American men nuts. Anyone care to wager on what the Gulf War did to the fragile male psyche? War is hell, Marvin Gaye sang to a nation, and it don't matter which war we are scrutinizing. I lived in New York City one year when over two thousand of my fellow citizens—disproportionately young Black men—were murdered at the height of the crack wars. War is hell, indeed.

And no less hellish is the war of going inward to unearth some excruciating truths versus lashing outward at anyone within reach. Simply examine the scores of angry White males—young and old—the past several years, who have let loose with guns and bombs at schools, malls, religious edifices, federal buildings, places of employment, and elsewhere because they are clueless as to who they are and how they should function in this society. So they resort to what they have been taught to convey their dissatisfactions: the language and behavior of violence, not considering who may get caught in the crossfire of their emotional and spiritual underdevelopment. White men cannot remain immune to the contradictions embedded in the American definition of manhood.

Look at the characters who inhabit the classic fables of the ordinary American man we have been bombarded with for years: Sinclair Lewis' *Babbitt*, Arthur Miller's landmark play *Death of a Salesman*, Ernest Borgnine's portrayal of a Bronx butcher in the 1955 film *Marty*, Jackie Gleason's hotheaded shuffle as Ralph Kramden, Kevin Spacey's star turn as Lester Burnham in the lavishly feted *American Beauty*. Nearly every single time we get a depiction of the "ordinary American male," he is White, depressed, anxious, unhappy with his lot, and wedged in the towering weeds of his mundane environs. His misery and self-loathing make the lives of those around him unbearable. That, to me, is *extra*ordinary: that a man's life can be dictated to him from the moment he's told he's a man. He is born, goes to school, participates in one religious function or another, finishes school, goes to work, gets married and has a family, struggles to achieve the American dream (the house, the dog, the car, the latest appliances), and gets to sit at home and watch sports, drink beer, eat junk food, and gain weight. He can also, from the vantage point of his diminishing prospects, compare his life to the prosperous White men ceaselessly in the public eye: Donald Trump, Ted Turner, and Bill Gates on one hand, and the carefully manicured White Hollywood princes like Tom Cruise on the other, men who have a flair for life and a gusto he can touch only by way of his remote control. He feels, as Brando's Terry Malloy felt in *On the Waterfront*, that he could have been a contender, he could have been somebody, but what he *is* is a cog in someone else's well-oiled machine, there until he is put out to pasture (oh, those retirement communities) to die another day, bit by bit.

Perhaps this vapidness clarifies why so many so-called ordinary White males, down through history to the present, have embraced aspects of Black male posturing as a way of locating and identifying themselves. Could it be that what *they* have been given is so bare, so soulless, so sexless, so shallow that *they* have no choice but to venture beyond their cultural barriers, to cease being White and slip into the cultural personalities of their Black brothers? Well, how else does one explain the nineteenth-century spectacle of White men donning blackface, Black vernacular, and Black mannerisms for those minstrel shows? Or the mad dash to Harlem in the 1920s, after hours, to take in the "jungle music" and "prehistoric" mores of those untamed, uninhibited uptown residents? Did the legendary George Gershwin, he who gave us *Porgy and Bess* among many other songs and performance pieces clearly "borrowed" from Black life, feel so ordinary as a White male and so unsatisfied with what White American culture had to offer that he had to look elsewhere for that spark, that boost? Or, in the 1950s, did the simultaneous White male embrace of jazz and rock and roll, two art forms manufactured by Black hands, mean that America, in spite of having just won World War II, in spite of its love affair with White war icons, White Hollywood icons, and even its icons in that new medium called television, leave something to be desired for the ordinary American White male? Recall that Norman Mailer's famous essay "The

White Negro" was published in the postwar era of un-matched American power and detailed the White desire to be something other than one's White self; that White men, in search of that cultural high, could go "slummin'" in the Black ghettos if they had to. And clearly, Elvis Presley, he of the Negro blues and gospel influences, the swiveling hips, and the Black vocal inflections, would not have been given the carte blanche bestowed upon him had he not been a country-ass White boy imitating Black boys, and doing so well enough to make White girls swoon and cash registers sing. In the 1970s we got the Bee Gees, whom I still dig as a group (they *could* sing and they *could* write the hell out of a song), mimicking the sweet sounds of soul singers like Eddie Kendricks of the Temptations, and that mimicry culminated in the astronomical success of *Saturday Night Fever,* both the film and the sound track. An essentially Black art form, disco, which was noth-ing more than watered-down soul music, made megastars of the Bee Gees and John Travolta (boy, did I *worship* Travolta as a preteen). And was not John Travolta's Italian American working-class hero in *Saturday Night Fever* in essence doing dances originated by Black and Brown male bodies, both straight and gay, in places like Harlem years before?

The point I am making is this: The White male, just like the Black male and all other males in America since America has been America, has been in this perpetual search for himself, for the *it* that will tell him who he is. Thus, when I see an Eminem jump upon the scene with his wounded White male swagger, I am not surprised that he is a very good rapper, is a very good lyricist, and, really, has the talent, the way Benny Goodman, Elvis, the Righteous Brothers, the Bee Gees, and Hall and Oates did before him, to pull off a blue-eyed, blond-haired version of Black manliness. Nope, not surprised at all. What is funny, though—and not in that ha-ha way—is that Eminem's success ironically illustrates the persistent gap between the possibilities offered by White and Black manhood. While Eminem is given the space to be angry, to cuss, to scream, to carry a gun, to get arrested, to reveal the lurid scar of his life prior to his incredible fame and wealth, to be an asshole, to dis women, to dis gays and lesbians, to dis publicly his momma (something most Black men, no matter how much some of us hate Black women, would never do), and to dis his baby's momma, Eminem is still treated like a human being, as a member of the family. On the other hand, most Black rappers—like, say, Tupac Shakur in his lifetime—are depicted as deranged and hazardous, are marginalized, and are regarded as public enemy number one. Most things wrong with the American social fabric—sexism, violence, materialism—are attributed to this Black male, as if Black males are somehow more devious than White males. The media and pop culture engine surely reinforces that perception every single day. And yeah, sure, Eminem has faced a barrage of criticism. But there is something different here, as measured by the fact that Em's career has actually accelerated in spite of all the controversies, to the point that he has now been embraced as a genius, an artist and American icon, in spite of the fact that he is not, no matter what anyone tries to tell me, the best rapper ever to emerge. Not even close.

It all goes back to how White-skin privilege operates in America, especially for White males. You are allowed that freedom to wild out, go off, act a fool, and you are given the freedom to come back to the fold, to *embody* the fold. Fact is, there was a time when Elvis was an outsider to many, and now he is the king of rock and roll. There was a time when Beat writer Jack Kerouac, who jacked Black culture as much as he could for creative inspiration, was considered a pariah by mainstream America, and now he is seen as one of the geniuses of American letters. There was a time when George W. Bush was a carousing, drinking fool straight outta the flick *Animal House*, and now magically he is president of the United States. And so it goes, and so it will go for Eminem, as evidenced by the enormous box office and sound track success of his first film, *8 Mile*.

In *8 Mile* Eminem plays an ordinary young White male named Rabbit whose only way out of his mundane existence, at a Detroit-area factory by day and in what appears to be a trailer community by night, is to conquer the wild terrain of MC battles, which, not so coincidentally, are largely populated by Black males. Cleverly based on strands of Em's real life, *8 Mile* has a number of foils for Rabbit: the emotionally abusive mother, the live-in boyfriend no older than Rabbit, and the young sister who puts us in mind of Hailie, Em's real-life daughter and the only person on the planet he seems to love. *8 Mile* is supposed to suggest the separation of Black and White communities in Detroit, but the film would lead us to believe that there is nonstop racial mixing: Most of Rabbit's friends, save his dim-witted White friend Cheddar Bob, are Black. Rabbit's overbearing boss is a loudmouthed, short-tempered Black man. Rabbit's connection to a possible record demo is a hustling Black man. Rabbit's homeboy, played by Mekhi Phifer in a ridiculously hideous dreadlock wig, is Black. Phifer's character seems to believe in Rabbit more than he believes in himself, and it was not lost on me when Em, uh, I mean Rabbit, suggested in one of his freestyle rhymes that Phifer's character was an Uncle Tom. And, of course, Rabbit's tormentors/rap competition are all thugged-out, gangsterish, and utterly treacherous Black men. There is not one Black male character in *8 Mile* who is as fully developed as Rabbit, bearing the sort of redeeming qualities that historically have made the ordinary White guy such a lovable figure, from James Stewart to Tom Hanks. Rabbit is a thinker, Rabbit is sensitive, Rabbit is ambitious, Rabbit is relatively naive and innocent, and Rabbit, unlike everyone around him, does not want to be stuck at the bottom. In short, Rabbit can see his way out of the hole. And he sees MCing, or rapping, as his ticket to the promised land. Think Rocky Balboa meets Tarzan meets the bullet-riddled hip-hop world after Tupac Shakur and the Notorious B.I.G. and you get the picture. Suffice it to say that *8 Mile* is an extremely mediocre movie that co-opted the implausible popularity of the first major White rapper since Vanilla Ice. That Vanilla Ice was not really taken seriously by a lot of Black and White people, although a lot of Black and White people did buy millions and millions of Vanilla Ice's records. But Vanilla Ice did not fit the mold of a talented White person who could appeal to Black people (the true litmus test), his own people, and other people. Vanilla Ice was no ordinary American male; he was an ordinary faker. Eminem, on the other hand, is indelibly authentic and speaks very much to the alienation, angst, and rage of young White people, particularly young White males. He has enough bravado and talent and clever rhyme schemes to bring Black young people along for the ride. And because Eminem is White and all that word means, he has a special brand of skin privilege that a Tupac Shakur, an Ice Cube, Rakim, a Slick Rick, and dozens of other equally talented or more talented rappers never had. So, like Elvis before him, Eminem gets to be, even if it is not his intention, the new (White) face of hip-hop, and really a continuation of the ideology of White supremacy. In the case of hip-hop it goes like this: *You Negroes have literally destroyed this culture, so we now have someone to save it who is a lot safer (or at least safer-looking) than the perilous Black male figure who has been invading our children's bedrooms for years, and he may even one day clean up his act and become a model citizen or, rather, one of us.* It does not matter that Eminem is nowhere near as talented an actor as Tupac Shakur was, or that *8 Mile* does not come close to packing the emotional punch of *Juice,* or *Boyz 'N the Hood,* or *Menace II Society,* for that matter. What matters, still, is how race functions in America, and how White males, even the ordinary and ostracized ones, get to come out on top in the end if they wind up in the right situation. This was evident as I sat in the theater not once but three times taking in *8 Mile*, my mind's eye surveying the racial mix of the audience. The White youth in attendance clearly, somewhere in their minds, relished the opportunity to identify with one of their own. The youth of color, most of whom probably are as confused about race and racism as I was as a shorty, loved Eminem because they were told to do so by the marketing machine, which meshes neatly with the ideology of White supremacy they get in school anyhow. With the aforementioned Black hip-hop films I listed a few lines ago, 99 percent of the audiences I was a part of were Black. And in each of those Black hip-hop films Black men get killed, usually one of the principal characters. In *8 Mile* Rabbit not only triumphs over the wild terrain of the MC battle after battling his own fears and inner demons (as Tarzan did in those steamy jungles), but at the film's end we are left to believe that Rabbit has passed a serious test by whupping the Black boys at their own game. Now he can march through the alley and on to the promised land, the same promised land that Elvis found. Damn homie, the hip-hop Tarzan meets Elvis.

And recall how in those omnipresent ads for Elvis' most recent collection of hits, an announcer proclaims, disrespectfully and despicably, that *before anyone did anything, Elvis did everything*. Which is blatantly asserting that Big

Mama Thornton, Chuck Berry, Little Richard, Ike Turner, Louis Jordan, Bo Diddley, B. B. King, and a whole multitude of Black rockers did not exist, were invisible, have been forgotten, or have been wiped from the history pages of some folks' racist minds—if the pages were ever there in the first place. Will there come a day when Eminem will be elevated past Run-DMC, Rakim, Ice Cube, Scarface, Big Daddy Kane, Kool G Rap, Chuck D., Slick Rick, Mos Def, Common, the Notorious B.I.G., and Tupac Shakur, and hailed as the greatest MC of all time, as the king of rap? As long as the ideology of White supremacy and White-skin privilege thrives, history tells us the answer is a resounding yes, particularly if White males with no sense of history, politics, race, race relations, racism, freedom, justice, and equality get to tell and write the stories. And if Black people, duped into believing that Jesus Christ was White, that Columbus discovered America, that Lincoln wanted to free the slaves without any severe reservations, and that Bill Clinton was the first Black president (how offensive a statement), cannot see that the coronation of Eminem as the best rapper of this era is part and parcel of a wicked commodification of hip-hop, the same sort of commodification that had Pat Boone and Ricky Nelson covering Black tunes in the 1950s or groups like the Rolling Stones interpolating as much blues (right down to the band's name) as they could get their hands on in the 1960s, then some of us really have bought into the big lie that the American empire became a democracy after the Civil Rights Movement, and that is simply not the case.

America remains a work in progress. I personally can admit I have had many influences in my life, some Black, some White, some Latino, some Asian, some Native American, all of them human. What I think is missing from the discussion around race and racism in America is an awareness that things have never been balanced, that things have always been tilted toward the White side, the White perspective. Some of us darker sisters and brothers are simply sick and tired of being sick and tired of business as usual.

WHEN I TALK about Tupac Shakur, with all his smarts and all his self-defeating inconsistencies, I often find myself defensive because I recall how vicious the media has been in its depiction of Black men. I will be the first to stand on line and shout that brothers like Mike Tyson, O. J. Simpson, and Suge Knight strike me as being deeply disturbed. But are they any more disturbed than the American empire that gave birth to them? Or are they merely acting out their roles as its native sons? At his finest, Tupac Shakur was one of the most sensitive and vulnerable men I have ever met. At his worst, he was vile and malicious, someone whose dictionary skipped words like *poise* and *control*. But that is what happens when one lives in a society where being a sensitive and vulnerable male is not rewarded. Tupac did not stand a chance, not really.

Tupac also had the misfortune to come of age in an industry controlled by a handful of major record labels who in the name of the bottom line were busy reducing the imagery of young Black men to the most narrow and violent range ever. This was not always the case in hip-hop, but Tupac's entrance into the industry came at a time of dramatic flux.

When Tupac entered the music business, with the Bay Area's Digital Underground in the late 1980s, there was no such thing as positive rap and negative rap, conscious rap and unconscious rap, or even underground rap and commercial rap. It was all rap: the spoken-word aspect of the larger hip-hop culture. During that period, a time we hip-hop heads now refer to fondly as the golden era of hip-hop (roughly 1987–1993), not only was there a diversity of Black male voices and styles (Public Enemy, Too Short, Geto Boys, Young MC, and others coexisted for the most part peacefully), but there was a diversity of opinions on what Black manhood could be. This was a result of so many young Black men finding their voices at once in this culture they'd grown up with. Remarkably, there was a window of opportunity in which this full spectrum of voices—of lives—could be expressed. Which means that the average young Black kid had options for emulation: If you were into the street thing, you could roll with Kool G Rap and DJ Polo or N.W.A.; if you were into the political thing, you could roll with Public Enemy or XClan; if you were into having a good time, you could roll with Tone-Loc or Kid 'N Play; if you were into the flower-child bohemian thing, you could roll with De La Soul or A Tribe Called Quest; and if you wanted a middle-class prankster, you could roll with DJ Jazzy Jeff and the Fresh Prince. All of it was rap, all of it was hip-hop, and all of it was representative of the state of Black manhood during that time.

Digital Underground, a bunch of fun-loving partiers, had a massive hit with "The Humpty Dance" during the Golden Era. Although Tupac did not rap on that song, there is video footage of Tupac dancing onstage with a blow-up doll, which was a far cry from the Tupac Shakur who would become legendary as the progenitor of the thug-life philosophy. By the early 1990s, I submit, music industry power brokers (the folks who write and sign the checks) had grown weary and fearful of the potential explosiveness of the Black nationalism saturating hip-hop, as led by Public Enemy and its frontman Chuck D., since it was not only educating Black and Latino young people but deeply affecting White youth as well. White kids who had previously learned little or nothing about Black history could now listen to Boogie Down Productions' "You Must Learn" and in a four-minute song get more Black American and American history than they would get in twelve or thirteen years of school. At the same time, by the early 1990s the proliferation of crack cocaine and guns in inner cities across America was sending thousands of young Black males to jail and premature graves, and this new stage of violence in urban America began to make its way into hip-hop music and culture. Nothing wrong with that, because hip-hop has always been Black America's CNN, as Chuck D. famously put it. And, truth be told, many of the brothers who had gotten fat from hustling drugs needed a legitimate angle, and flipping dirty money into a lawful business is as American as apple pie, as American as Joseph Kennedy flipping bootleg liquor money into political power, culminating in the election of his son John F. Kennedy to the presidency of the United States (and John's brother Bobby ironically following along as attorney general).

In addition to the drug epidemic, there were two major events in 1992 and 1993 that accelerated this change in hip-hop: the so-called Los Angeles riots of 1992 and the release of Dr. Dre's *The Chronic* in 1993. The L.A. riots, from my ghetto viewpoint, epitomized the frustration of Black people, especially poor Black men, with the remote and arbitrary power of the system. Remember, the riots were a reaction to an all-White jury pronouncing that the White police officers who had been caught on videotape beating motorist Rodney King were not guilty of the very thing all of America and the world saw them doing on video. And remember that the Black community in South Central waited out the judicial process, over a year, before reacting, still believing, against all of history's evidence, that justice would be served. So the Black community of South Central Los Angeles did what Chuck D. had urged a few years before: They were fighting the power in their own way.

The Chronic, a seductively produced classic hip-hop album, also epitomized what was wrong with post-civil-rights Black America. After it sold several million copies to Black and White kids across the country, *The Chronic* became the music industry's blueprint for hip-hop music from that point on: lots of senseless gunplay and violence, cursing ad nauseam, the liberal use of self-hating terms like *nigga* and *bitch,* an insatiable appetite for marijuana, liquor, and sex, and an incredible disrespect and disregard for Black women. In retrospect, Negro voices like C. Delores Tucker, the Reverend Calvin Butts, Wynton Marsalis, and Stanley Crouch were not all that wrong about *some* aspects of hip-hop. My problem with them folks was, and is, their political and personal motives and their gross disconnect from the culture and from the young people who constitute the hip-hop community nationwide. If you are not engaged in something fully, if you do not have a level of compassion for the people who have created the thing you are so critical of, then you have a sharply limited amount of credibility and might better serve with silence. But hip-hop is my culture: I grew up with it and in it. And the fact is that after *The Chronic* in particular, hip-hop was redirected, co-opted, commodified, and exploited to the point where it has become a modern-day minstrel show complete with platinum chains, expensive name-brand clothing, high-priced automobiles, and a severe abhorrence of Black self.

Of course, the so-called hip-hop purists will argue that we need to make a distinction between hip-hop culture and the hip-hop industry, that the industry is corrupt but the culture remains pure. Granted, homies, but the reality is that most of the young heads I lecture to, in the 'hoods, in prisons, on college campuses, wherever, ain't even thinking about no hip-hop culture these days. To them a Snoop Dogg or a Jay-Z or a Nelly or a 50 Cent is as good as it gets and *is* hip-hop, straight up, no chaser, whether purists like it or not.

Other people complain that folks like me are holding hip-hop to a higher standard than any other pop cultural phenomenon: We don't require rock-and-roll musicians, for instance, to provide "positive" images to kids, do we, much less teach history and spark revolution? But hip-hop was not born just to become another cog in American capitalism; hip-hop was created as a voice for the kids left behind. Hip-hop has always had higher potential and thus greater accountability when it comes up short. And its fans have always been more vulnerable to negative images. Think about the fact that much of the American school system, be it public schools or private schools, never ceased presenting education from the perspective of the White male power structure, in spite of the civil rights era and the feminist movement. This means that many of the young people in this country, Black, White, and otherwise, still learn little or nothing about the Black contributions to American society other than Crispus Attucks' death to kick off the American Revolution, Harriet Tubman's Underground Railroad, Booker T. Washington's work in education, Rosa Parks' protest on that Alabama bus, and Dr. King's "I have a dream" speech. And even this list is a stretch given some of the places I have visited, including some of the so-called finest educational institutions in America.

This is real basic, y'all: If you do not learn about yourself, you are not going to like yourself. In fact, you more than likely will grow to hate yourself and people who look like you. If you aren't taught any better, then you'll see nothing wrong with referring to yourself and people who look like you as "niggas" and "bitches" and "ghetto" and all the other self-hating things we hear in these dark days. Given how bankrupt much of the school system is in terms of presenting American history from the perspective of all people, it logically follows that young people (as had been the case with me when I was coming of age) wind up turning to other arenas for their knowledge base: the streets, the playground, the neighborhood, the radio, the television. And given that hip-hop is now a multi-billion-dollar industry and *the* dominant youth culture on the planet today, it has become one of the chief ways young people learn about life in America's ghettos and, by extension, about the great Black majority. It has also become a lever that young Black people pull to process their own experiences, a reflection to help them make sense of their own lives and condition. Hip-hop culture certainly did not create ghettos, poverty, self-hatred, violence, crime, sexism, materialism, extreme individualism, hedonism, ignorance, or any of that. Indeed, those themes and those realities existed in the Black worlds of blues, jazz, rhythm and blues, rock and roll, and soul long before hip-hop's rise to the top of the heap. And we certainly know that White rockers, ranging from Mick Jagger and Keith Richards of the Rolling Stones, to the punk idols, the Ramones, to Guns 'n Roses, certainly have produced their share of sexism and misogyny, violence and mayhem, and drug and liquor orgies, not only in their music, but in their personal lives.

But the problem with hip-hop today is that there is no balance in the conversation, no broadness in the dialogue we call rap. So when the music and culture have been reduced to discussing only the most negative aspects of ghetto life in a way that glorifies them, then that becomes the way many young Black people will begin to think about their own lives and experiences. It will also have an effect on what outsiders on cultural safaris (all the White youth in America who love hip-hop) will think of Black people: that we are nothing more than a bunch of materialistic, sex-crazed, weed-smoking, gun-toting, brand-name-wearing "niggas" and "bitches" with bad attitudes. In a sense, beloved, the very poor people Dr. King was so concerned about near the end of his life, the very poor people who created hip-hop as a way to be alive, have had hip-hop snatched from them, turned inside out, and sold back to them in the form of the worst aspects of their lives. Hip-hop was created as a way of living, breathing, *being*. Now it has become about gagging, dying, and disappearing.

But who is to blame for its demise, for its arrested development? The easy thing to do, as we tend to do in this society, is to blame the folks at the bottom, the most powerless, namely, the folks in America's ghettos or the rap artists themselves. Fact is, folks in the ghetto are basically surviving day to day and doing whatever it takes to eat and pay the bills. Fact is, most young rap artists, most young *Black* rap artists, unless they happen to have a parent or parents like Afeni Shakur, are, more times than not, completely oblivious to American and Black American history and are just trying to make the records they think will sell and get them out of the ghetto as fast as possible. What they see and hear is selling is what the multinational record labels, the multinational video channels, and the monopolized radio stations are putting forth on a daily basis. What is a poor cat to do if he is told, and comes to believe, that the only way he will be able to cease being a ghetto bastard is to become like the stars in the firmament of heavy rotation? He will believe he must begin to think of himself as a nigga and the women in his life as bitches, he must learn to worship platinum chains, diamonds, fur coats, and late-model automobiles, he must become addicted to two-ways and Xbox and high-priced liquor, and he must have no care in the world beyond what is on the radio, in the music videos, and at the record stores. That is a formula, a recipe, for living the lifestyle of the 'hood rich and ghetto fabulous. But it's also a formula for the destruction of an entire generation.

When Russell Simmons held his inaugural Hip-hop Summit in New York City in June 2001, it was tagged as "Taking Back Responsibility." It should have been called "Who's Gonna Take the Weight?" because, save Russell, it seems that most of the folks in a position to effect serious change for hip-hop ain't trying to do *nada*. I have been in and around the entertainment industry for approximately seventeen years, and I am telling you it is downright depressing to see the writers, the publicists, the label executives, the radio folks, and the television people all act as if nothing is wrong with hip-hop, as if we don't collectively have to share some responsibility for allowing it to be co-opted and dumbed down to where it is currently. And I am doubly depressed by the *Black* writers, the *Black* publicists, the *Black* label executives, the *Black* radio folks, and the *Black* television people, many of whom are college-educated and middle-class and should *know better*, but do not, or do not care, or think (as many Whites do) that those ghetto niggas are just a bunch of animals anyhow. Meanwhile, these college-educated, middle-class Black folks are making careers and money on the backs of their less fortunate and less educated sisters and brothers. Which leads me back to integration and what it did to our sense of a collective and common struggle. In this day and age, when it is all about the benjamins and survival of the fittest, how can one be fit if one has not been given the resources, the skills, the education, and the opportunity to be fit?

More obnoxious still is to hear some of these cats justify what they are doing. I was at a Congressional Black Caucus panel in September 2002 organized by Congresswoman Maxine Waters that was supposed to be about the business side of hip-hop but had more to do with gratuitously patting panelists Russell Simmons, Andre Harrell, and Island Def Jam bigwig Kevin Lyles on the back for being smart enough to make mucho bucks in an integrated America. It was Lyles who particularly got my goat. This man, who helps to distribute the music of artists like Jay-Z, Ludacris, and Ja Rule, said he saw nothing wrong with the music, nothing wrong with the fact that the money he is making allows him to live in whatever community he wants, for his kids to not be boxed in by "Blackness," and for his kids to go to the best schools. Another question begs itself: Well, what about the Black kids in the ghettos of America who buy and listen to Jay-Z, Ludacris, and Ja Rule, all artists affiliated with Island Def Jam, who are born and more than likely will die in the 'hood, where police harassment and police brutality remind them daily, weekly, yearly, that they are Black, and where the schools they attend are overcrowded and peppered with inefficiencies? *Does he even care?* I wondered as I listened to Kevin Lyles pontificate, on and on, till the break of dawn, unchecked by Congresswoman Waters, who had a mic and was essentially moderating the panel. What was *she* thinking, given that a large segment of the district she represents in Los Angeles, including South Central L.A., is exactly what I just described? And was it not Rep. Waters who once protested that the CIA purposely brought crack cocaine into Black communities? Then she must somehow see the connection between the crack cocaine epidemic that was unleashed on the Black community by outside forces to devastating effect and the music and culture that is similarly exploited for profit by the multinational record companies and the radio station monopolies to devastating effect.

Again, hip-hop did not create any of the ghetto conditions, the self-hatred, the sexism, or the violence that we currently see in vogue, and it is wrong and idiotically simplistic for archconservatives like Bill O'Reilly to scapegoat hip-hop for many of America's social ills. Fact is, America was founded on hatred, sexism, violence, and a laundry list of things that are immoral and inhumane. But a lot of hip-hop today is a drug that induces capitulation to those ghetto conditions. If, like a drug dealer or a drug cartel, you keep pushing the same product every day, the same ten or twelve songs every hour every day on the radio, you are going to hook people, and the mentalities will change to reflect what is being pushed to them, to what is being perpetuated. It is a lie, a myth, to say that the record labels and the radio stations and the magazines and the television outlets are giving the people what they want. On the contrary, the power brokers determine what the people should request, then make the people think that they are asking for it of their own accord. It is called marketing, my friend. I've seen how it works from inside of the industry matrix.

By the time Tupac's career was ready to step off, much of hip-hop became about life in the ghetto, not only describing it but glorifying it. I remember well how one of Ice Cube's early albums, *AmeriKKKa's Most Wanted*, had a "life" side and a "death" side. Yes, rappers have always been street reporters, but Cube's point is that it was not enough to present the griminess and madness in the ghetto without also putting forth some solutions and some sense of hope and possibility. If you look back over the body of Tupac Shakur's work, there are many songs that deal with the highs and lows of inner-city dwelling, songs that are overtly political and songs that care about nothing more than smoking weed, drinking, sexing women, and having a good time. That is the yin and the yang of humanity. At a certain point in hip-hop's partnership with corporate America humanity went the way of the buffalo, yo. Tupac himself told me that "thug life," his grab-you-by-the-collar moniker for the movement he wanted to build for Black men in America's gutters, was supposed to be political, but his record label chieftans encouraged him to "keep it real" and "keep it street" because the political stuff was not selling anymore. Well, why had the political stuff stopped selling? Was it simply the end of a trend, or had the plug been pulled? Why not connect the dots, beloved?

How did we go from righteous and bold images of Malcolm X and Martin Luther King Jr. and the Black Panther Party in the 1960s to everyone wanting to be a silky-tongued, ghetto-fabulous pimp, thanks to films like *The Mack* and *Superfly* in the early 1970s? How did we go from admiration for a Chuck D. and his audacious voice to an admiration for any rapper who calls himself a nigga and *any* woman within reach of his tongue a bitch? When you really deconstruct hip-hop music videos today, a striking similarity emerges with the buffoonish minstrelsy of yesteryear. Back in the day we bugged our eyes, poked out our lips, shuffled and jived, danced and pranced, and enunciated our words in a way that made it clear we were obsequious, boot-licking coons obsessed with eating, sleeping, drinking, sexing, and having a good time. This is how the

Hollywood factory manufactured us, and this is how we were projected out to the world. Today we bug and roll our eyes, poke out our lips, shuffle and jive with expensive bottles of champagne in our hands, dance and prance as if we are making a porno film, and enunciate our words in a way that makes it clear we are some obsequious, boot-licking coons obsessed with eating, sleeping, drinking, sexing, and having a good time. This is how the five major record companies that control much of the world's music manufacture us, and again, this is how we are projected out to the world and back to ourselves. I'ma say it again: Save the Native American, what other people in America's long and twisted voyage across the bumpy roads of race and racism have been depicted in such a fashion and for so long, quite literally reducing the men to pimps and the women to whores? For sure, what were once the subcultures and peripheral images of Black manhood, namely the pimp and the gangsta, are now *the* culture and *the* image for all of us, boys from the block, and college boys on the yard, thugs united and madly misguided.

I'VE THOUGHT ABOUT these issues a great deal since those sad moments when I was in Las Vegas covering what would be the last days of Tupac Shakur's tragic story for *Rolling Stone*. It was otherworldly because up until that week, I had written about Tupac exclusively for *Vibe* magazine. But because I had been fired four months prior, I was now on assignment for another magazine. No matter; I knew I needed to be in Las Vegas. Why? I am not exactly sure. When I arrived in Vegas, three days before Tupac died, I said to myself that this was not the type of city in which I wanted to die. There are slot machines even at the airport, and you can literally get anything you want on the Strip: sex, drugs, cars, a lawyer, a marriage, or a divorce. It is little wonder Las Vegas is called "Sin City." As I made my way around town, talking with cabdrivers, hotel maids, construction workers, card table operators, prostitutes, police officers, and others, it was clear that few knew or even cared to know about the life and times of Tupac Shakur.

Some thought he was a gangsta. Others thought he was a gang member (some said he was a Blood, others said he was a Crip). Many also said that Tupac's getting shot in Las Vegas brought unnecessary attention to a city already dogged by a seedy image. The more I explored Las Vegas (I couldn't do much else until the day Tupac actually died because Suge Knight's security team—or whoever they were—made sure that the media and other unknowns did not come too close to the hospital), the more I thought of Nicolas Cage's Academy Award–winning role in *Leaving Las Vegas*. Hadn't Cage's character, an outcast, come to Las Vegas to die? Hadn't Cage's character succumbed to alcohol addiction and taken up with prostitutes? Hadn't Cage's character given up on life? How many times, I asked myself, had Tupac Shakur said to me he would not live a long time, that he in fact did not want to live a long time, and that he would probably go down in a hail of bullets? The thought of the fast-moving world of Las Vegas being a burial ground for those who had lived fast lives, like Tupac, unnerved me. Maybe, as many of his fans have suggested, Tupac did see it coming and knew when and where he was going to die. Hadn't he achieved his very modest goals of "hearing myself on a record and seeing myself in a movie"? What else was there for him to live for if he was, as he said so often, in so much pain? So much pain, he maintained, that only his huge intake of weed allowed him to live as long as he had.

When I listen to some of the comments about Tupac Shakur specifically, and about young Black men in America's inner cities in general, it is clear that many of those commenting are very much out of touch with reality. It is so easy to say, for example, "Well, Tupac had choices" or "Tupac knew what he was getting himself into." What choices, really, did Tupac have? He was born poor, so he knew he had to survive. While middle-class White and Black children have the option of thinking about what they want to do with their lives, Tupac decided early on that being a rapper was his surest and perhaps only ticket out of the ghetto. And in the insulated world of ghetto culture, your Blackness, your manhood, are narrowly defined by how "real" you keep it, how hard you are, how much you represent the thug life. Move one step away from that and you are considered a sellout. And why would Tupac Shakur—who had been an outcast his entire life, who resented that when he was a child his cousins said he was "too pretty"—position himself in any other way except as a "real nigga"? That does not suggest choice; it suggests doing what you have to do to survive in the ghetto world that produced you. Sure, Tupac could have assimilated easily into the realm of Hollywood (he did hang out with the likes of Madonna and Mickey Rourke), but that plastic, middle-class existence meant nothing to him. Nor was it real. What was real were the homies, from South Central Los Angeles to the South Bronx, whom he felt he had to represent. So when you think of Tupac—the baggy pants with the boxer shorts peeking out, the numerous tattoos, the bald head, the bandanna, the pimp limp, the jewelry, the women, the mouth, the attitude—you are essentially getting the average working-class Black male in America today. And last time I checked, there are more of us than the bourgeois variety we are told by some to be like. From the bebop era of Dizzy Gillespie and Charlie Parker to hip-hop, Black men have always rebelled against the customs of the larger society through their art and their lives, through their *beings*. People like to say hip-hop is just so harsh, so foul. Well, as Amiri Baraka once famously put it, you can always tell the station of a people by the music and culture they produce at any given time. To blame hip-hop and the Tupac Shakurs of the world for what is wrong with Black youth is to ignore the blood on your own hands. Some of the more wishful among us like to say that Tupac Shakur could have been "our next Malcolm." Again, that kind of statement speaks to our fascination with icons and our propensity for deifying people who breathe and sleep and bleed and defecate just like the rest of us. Moreover, as far as I am concerned, the question is not whether Tupac Shakur would have been the next Malcolm X had he lived, but whether Malcolm Little would have become Malcolm X had he been born today. In other words, there is no organization or movement in place that could reach out to the Tupac Shakurs of America and uplift them the way the Nation of Islam did with Malcolm (those who believe the NOI today is what it was then must be on crack). Tupac, like many of us who are young, Black, and male, was pretty much out there on his own. Who was giving him direction? And who understood *fully* what he was going through? Not his mother. Not his family. Not his friends. Not his fans. Not his enemies. Not Suge Knight. Perhaps not even Tupac himself. And not his father, whoever that was.

On the evening of Tupac's death I drove with my journalist friend to the intersection of Flamingo Road and Koval Lane, where Tupac had been shot. As my friend called in her story I just stared at that intersection, wondering why there were no witnesses in such a well-lit and heavily traveled area. I called my homegirl Tracy Carness in Los Angeles, and her first words to me, before we could even exchange greetings, were "Kevin, he's dead. I can't believe he is dead." Neither could I. Tupac was, in a phrase, a "bad nigga." That scared a lot of people, and excited just as many. I was, through the years, somewhere in the middle. I was not scared of Tupac. I was scared for him. But I also loved the fact that he had no problem throwing up his middle finger anywhere and anytime it suited him. As he rapped once, "I was given this world, I didn't make it." And as far as Tupac was concerned, this world had been giving him and people who looked like him the finger all along. So Tupac's life was an exacting sort of revenge, on White people, on snobby Black people, on the rich, on anyone who had no sympathy for the oppressed and voiceless on this planet.

After I spoke with my friend Tracy, I went back to my hotel room, got drunk, poured some liquor on the carpet in Tupac's memory, and recalled the last time I'd seen him in person. It was late November 1995. Tupac had been bailed out of an upstate New York prison by Suge Knight (he had been incarcerated for a sexual assault charge stemming from that hotel room encounter with the young woman) and was now back in Los Angeles shooting a video for the new single from his double CD. The $600,000 "California Love" video was being shot a hundred miles north of Los Angeles at a dry lake bed in the desert. I milled around for a while checking out the imitation *Mad Max* set, then made my way to Tupac's trailer. I knocked on the door, and someone on the other side pushed it open, releasing a powerful gust of marijuana smoke. And there he was, the big eyes shining brightly, the smile still childlike and broad as an ocean, his exposed muscles—probably because of his eleven-month prison bid—bigger than ever. Clearly this was not the same Tupac who had, only ten months earlier while in jail, told me that he was no longer going to smoke weed, that he was not a gangsta, that "thug life is dead." Or maybe it was. Whatever the case, from that day in November until his death Tupac became in my mind an exact replica of the character he played in *Juice*. It was shocking to hear his new album, it was shocking to see him in television interviews, and it pissed me off that he helped to escalate the tensions between East Coast and West Coast rappers (born on the East Coast, Tupac had gone back and forth with his sentiments until he signed to Death Row Records in October 1995). For sure, when I asked Tupac what was going to come of the East Coast–West Coast rift, he said, as he was being whisked away to do a television interview, "It's gonna get deep." How prophetic were those words, as first Tupac and then the Notorious B.I.G. were blown away, both murders still unsolved all these years later. I watched Tupac for the next few hours as he shot scenes and paraded in front of cameras, counting wads of money, as the hulking persona of Suge Knight stood in the background.

A few weeks later I spoke to Tupac for the last time when I conducted a follow-up telephone interview with him. Apparently much had changed in Tupac's mind since our last interview, and he let it be known how angry he was, it seemed, with everyone. But, he maintained, he could at least trust Suge Knight and the Death Row family because they could protect him from his enemies. I remember hanging up the phone after that interview, on December 2, 1995, and feeling very sick. I know what it is to be angry because I have a very short fuse. And I know what it is to feel paranoid, to believe in your heart that no one is your friend and that everyone is out to get you. But Tupac displayed a side of himself that I had never seen, a darker, more menacing side. I thought, *Damn, maybe I never really knew him.* I didn't want to speak to Tupac Shakur anymore. I guess a part of me knew it was only a matter of time before he would get his wish and be gone from us forever. I never stopped following Tupac's life, and whenever I heard someone mention his name, I listened as carefully as I had done back in 1992. 'Pac once told me he wanted me to be Alex Haley to his Malcolm X, to be the official biographer of his life. And that is precisely how I felt at times, like the one writer who was attempting to present a broad picture of Tupac Shakur, who was making an effort to understand him because, hell, Tupac was me, and I was him, ghetto bastards from birth, living until it is our turn to die. So, in a way, the "new" Tupac made me feel as if I had lost a friend, and there was nothing I could do about it. He was gone.

I met Tupac's natural father, Billy Garland, a few weeks after Tupac died. Tupac had been so adamant about not knowing his father that I did not believe that this man was in fact his father until I saw him in person. But the moment I saw him, I knew he was: There was the tall, lean body, the flat-footed walk, the girlish eyelashes, the long nose, and, yeah, the bushy eyebrows. To be honest, I had mixed feelings about the meeting. While I was glad to meet the man Afeni Shakur had referred to in my first *Vibe* article on Tupac as "Billy," I thought of how long it had taken Billy to reconnect with his son. And that was only after he had seen Tupac in *Juice*. What, I wondered would have been different about Tupac's life had Billy been there?

What would have been the same? Did Billy become interested in his son only once he became famous and, presumably, rich? Did Billy realize Tupac had spent his entire twenty-five years searching for father figures in the form of teachers, street hustlers, fellow rappers like Ice-T and Chuck D., and men as different as Suge Knight and Quincy Jones? I didn't ask Billy Garland any of these questions, but they were definitely on my mind. No matter: I sat and talked with Billy Garland for two or three hours in his Jersey City apartment, about his life, about Tupac's life, and about his absence from Tupac's universe. Billy showed me pictures of himself with Tupac, of the letters 'Pac had written him from prison, of the many cards he had received since Tupac's untimely death. Tupac had barely known this man, I thought, just as I barely knew my father. Was Billy Garland one of those Black men I had described previously, one of the damaged souls from the civil rights era, an ex-Panther and now a broken-down warrior trying to get a grip on his life via his dead son? Billy even asked me if he should sue Afeni Shakur for half of the Tupac Shakur estate. I was both astounded and appalled. This man had really been nothing more than a drop of sperm, and now he wanted to reap the benefits of the money a dead rapper as iconic as Tupac was sure to bring in. But for some reason I was not angry with Billy Garland. A part of me understood exactly where he was coming from because, hell, he is a Black man in America and has nothing to show for it except a tiny apartment and a dead, famous son. Billy had had a hard life himself, in the 1970s and

1980s, as he struggled to come of age as Tupac was coming of age. There had been no blueprint for Billy Garland, just as there had been no blueprint for Tupac Shakur, or for me, for that matter. We were—are—simply thrown out there and told to swim, although most of us do not know how and are too terrified to learn.

But it is something to see older Black men as I do now, as a man myself. I will be completely candid here and say that I have carried around a great deal of resentment toward older Black men since my father disowned me when I was eight years old. Indeed, I have had little tolerance, little respect, and very little interest in what most of them have to say for themselves. It is the worst form of cowardice to bring a child into the world and then abandon that child either because you cannot cope or because you and the child's mother are not able to get along. How many Black boys and Black girls have had their emotional beings decimated by that father void? Certainly Tupac, and certainly me.

Perhaps it is for this reason that I cannot readily recall all that Billy Garland said to me on that day after he asked my advice about suing Afeni Shakur. I was disgusted and saw in him my father and my grandfather and my uncle, my mother's only brother, and undeniably I saw myself and what I could possibly become. The predictability horrified me, because I could hear the echoes of my mother's caveat from my childhood: *Don't be like your father.* But what did my mother mean, precisely? If not like him, then like whom? In seeking to raid Tupac's grave for dollars, Billy

Garland was showing the worst attributes of Black man-hood, but also of White manhood, of American manhood. So what would the alternative be? How does one break the vicious cycle, begun on the plantations, of Black man as stud, as Black male body forced to tend someone else's land and property, as Black man torn away from his family, moved to and fro, of Black man being beaten down to the point that his woman and his children no longer know his name? Again, what of slavery, which lasted 246 years and lingers still in the collective bosom of Black men in America, particularly since we were slaves a hundred years longer than we have been free? So how could I really be mad at Billy Garland—or at my father, for that matter—anymore? Garland, via Tupac's death, was getting more at-tention than he had ever gotten in his entire rotten life, and he needed Tupac's death to validate his existence. How twisted a concept! But it is true. And what of my father, that no-good do-for-nothing, as my mother often referred to him? I may never see the man again in my lifetime, don't care to, really, but I know that wherever he is, he is not free. He is wounded; he is, like many older Black men and like a lot of younger Black men, in a state of arrested devel-opment, suspended above the fiery coals of his unstable journey here in America. But, with all of my being, I have to muster the nerve to forgive him, my father, for impreg-nating my mother, for not being there at the hospital when I was born, for not marrying my mother and leaving her to the whims of the welfare agency, for only showing up spo-radically the first eight years of my life, for declaring to my mother on that damp, rainy day that she had lied to him, that I was not his child, that he would not give her a "near nickel" for me ever again. Oh, how I suffered, as Tupac suffered, without a male figure in my life, someone whose skin felt like mine, whose blood beat like mine, whose walk pounded the earth for answers, like mine. But alas, poor Tupac, it was not meant to be, and you are dead, and I am here, and we both have fathers, yet we both are also father-less. The only thing I can say at this moment in my life journey—because, unlike Tupac, I did get to make it past twenty-five, into my thirties—is that I have to stay alive any way I can, and I have to be my own father now.